9.50

**What God Thinks About Money**

# What God Thinks About Money

**Get God's Perspective and Tap
Into a New Realm of
Abundance**

## Dedication

Through much thought and deep conviction, I dedicate

this book to those whose courage has given me the faith

to write it...  I speak of those who were brave enough to stand

in the pulpits of this world and teach God's people about the

life of biblical abundance, stewardship, and responsibility.

It is because of their willingness to sacrifice their own reputa-

tions that God, by the power of the Holy Spirit and through

biblical principles, has been able to bless his people and

finance the Gospel throughout the ages.

Your life has rewarded me.


With deep humility...

Robb Thompson

What God Thinks About Money
Get God's Perspective and Tap Into a New Realm of Abundance

ISBN # 978-1606834282
Copyright 2011 Robb Thompson
Published by Harrison House
Tulsa, OK 74145

# TABLE OF CONTENT$

Introduction: Some Beginning Thoughts    ix

1    The Real Story    1

2    Slaves To A Stingy God    7

3    Imprisoned By Lack    15

4    God Shall Supply    27

5    The Origin Of The Poverty Doctrine    47

6    Rich Jesus: Myth Or Fact?    59

7    Abundance Promised    75

8    Look At Heaven    93

9    The Battle Within The Mind    111

10    Our Rightful Inheritance    133

11    Faithful Stewardship    147

12    A Fresh Start    163

Conclusion: Our One Ambition    177

About The Author    187

Stop Trying
To Apply
The Word
To Your Life,
And Begin
To Apply
Your Life
To The Word.

Introduction

# SOME BEGINNING THOUGHT$

When anyone mentions the words "prosperity" and "God" in the same sentence, people tend to get a bit uneasy. Okay, let me rephrase that, people either get very excited or intensely angry. It is a subject that has divided much of the church. You may hear people say, "Oh, they are preaching the prosperity gospel," or you may encounter those who have taken an ill-informed "vow of poverty." I am not sure where you stand, but I ask you this: Will you put down, for just a moment, your preconceived ideas and feelings, and sincerely take a closer look at what I am about to lay before you?

I am not asking you to adopt, believe or even adhere to that which I am writing. All I ask is that you examine it closely. Take your Bible, and as the Bereans, search and study to see if these things are so.

> These were more fair-minded than those in Thessalonica, in that they received the word with all readiness and searched the Scriptures daily to find out whether these things were so.
>
> **Acts 17:11**

I receive many letters from people concerning this all-so-controversial subject. Men and women are being laid off from their jobs, losing their homes, and watching their credit card debt soar to an all-time high. But, as believers, we can and must operate in a system other than the one that society provides. And it begins when we choose who we will believe. Not just WHAT we believe, but WHO.

I am sure you can attest that where you are today is a direct result of those you have chosen to believe, or to put it in a different way, those you have chosen to trust. We have all been burned, lied to, cheated and stolen from. We have trusted those who have hurt us and brought us truckloads full of pain. But on the flip side, we have also benefited from, and been blessed by, loved on and cared for by those whom we have chosen to trust and believe. Just because someone lied to us doesn't mean we can't trust any longer. It simply means that we must be cautious and purposeful about whom we trust.

I am not asking you to trust or believe me. I am challenging you to search the Scriptures. What does the Bible have to say when it comes to God and money? Am I using the Scriptures to support this book, or is this book a result of that which the Word of God states?

That is for you to decide.

We all have questions when it comes to the subject of prosperity. All of us face questions every day. Let's not pretend that we don't. But these questions, whatever they are, need to be answered, and the only way that they can properly and accurately be answered is through and by the Word of God.

## God's Word Provides
## Answers Before Questions Are Asked.

So, why I have written this book? My purpose is to hopefully provide you with accurate information, sound doctrine and the necessary ammunition to fight the spirit of poverty that is doing all it can do to hold you back from the wonderful future God has for you and yours.

If you are ready to discover what the Bible has to say about this greatly misunderstood subject, then I believe I can help. I have uncovered a treasure chest of keys, principles and insights that continue to transform lives, and I am excited about the opportunity to share them with you.

# Abundance Is The Reward Of The Sower, While Lack Is The Consequence Of The Hoarder.

# Chapter 1

# THE REAL $TORY

Over the years, people have either secretly or publicly wondered what I truly believe about this subject. If the truth were known, much of what people think I believe is either horribly misguided or completely untrue. The public has linked me to a set of beliefs that I don't even believe myself.

In many circles, the subject of prosperity certainly has been abused. I would be a fool to deny any such claim. But in order to avoid such abuse, I have chosen to embrace only that which I find to be written in God's Word concerning the subject, nothing more, nothing less.

> **For God, who said, "Light shall shine out of darkness," is the One who has shone in our hearts to give the Light of the knowledge of the glory of God in the face of Christ.**
> **2 Corinthians 4:6, NASB**

Now, I am sure that in the past, I have made enormous mistakes, and I am certain that in the future, I will make many, many more – certainly more than I would like. This is why you will not find me on the side of the "naysayers" or the immature and greedy.

You will discover me when you search the hidden places that few know about, with one desire, which is to embrace only that which I find that God has written in His Holy Word, our source of truth and inspiration.

> **Sanctify them through thy truth: thy word is truth.**
>
> **John 17:17,** *KJV*

> **All scripture is given by inspiration of God, and is prof-itable for doctrine, for reproof, for correction, for instruction in righteousness:**
>
> **2 Timothy 3:16,** *KJV*

People ignorantly and falsely believe that I'm a prosperity preacher. They say things like, "Prosperity is wrong and doesn't belong in the church," or "You should never talk about money in church." These are immature and ignorant words with which I strongly disagree.

It would be like me speaking out against sex because of the great abuse that people have had to endure. It would be foolish to do so. Sex is from God, and it is very unfortunate that, at times, people have abused it. He created it, and it is meant for pleasure as well as reproduction. The fact that it's been abused (through rape, incest, fornication, etc.) certainly doesn't make it wrong, does it?

I am uncertain how you personally define prosperity or where your definition formed its roots, but here is how I see the Scriptures clearly define it:

## Prosperity, Or Abundance, Is Being Able To Meet Your Needs With Some Left Over To Help Meet The Needs Of Others.

And God is able to make all grace abound toward you; that ye, always having all sufficiency in all things, may abound to every good work: (As it is written, He hath dispersed abroad; he hath given to the poor: his righteousness remaineth for ever. Now he that ministereth seed to the sower both minister bread for your food, and multiply your seed sown, and increase the fruits of your righteousness;)

2 Corinthians 9:8-10, *KJV*

There are three levels of life described in the Bible:

1. **Insufficiency** – not enough to meet your needs

2. **Sufficiency** – just enough to meet your needs

3. **Abundance** – more than enough to meet your own needs and something left over to help meet the needs of others

What is important to understand is **that the purpose of abundance is not to live in excessive wealth but to have more than enough provision for every work that God has called us to do.**

And one of the company said unto him, Master, speak to my brother, that he divide the inheritance with me. And he said unto him, Man, who made me a judge or a divider over you? And he said unto them, Take heed, and beware of covetousness: for a man's life consisteth not in the abundance of the things which he possesseth. And he spake a parable unto them, saying, The ground of a certain rich man brought

3

forth plentifully: And he thought within himself, saying, What shall I do, because I have no room where to bestow my fruits? And he said, This will I do: I will pull down my barns, and build greater; and there will I bestow all my fruits and my goods. And I will say to my soul, Soul, thou hast much goods laid up for many years; take thine ease, eat, drink, and be merry. But God said unto him, Thou fool, this night thy soul shall be required of thee: then whose shall those things be, which thou hast provided? So is he that layeth up treasure for himself, and is not rich toward God.

Luke 12:13-21, KJV

If the Body of Christ continues to refute that God desires for His people to prosper (in the Biblical sense), then who is going to pay for and support the spreading of the gospel?

How then shall they call on him in whom they have not believed? and how shall they believe in him of whom they have not heard? and how shall they hear without a preacher? And how shall they preach, except they be sent? as it is written, How beautiful are the feet of them that preach the gospel of peace, and bring glad tidings of good things!

Romans 10:14-15, KJV

It takes money to spread the gospel that we say we cherish so much. There are printing and shipping costs for Bibles, tracts, and other religious books and travel expenses for those who go throughout the world preaching the gospel. Money buys food, shelter, clothing, and medical care for people in need, and this opens the door for them to receive the gospel message. All of these avenues and resources require money, and lots of it.

Money is certainly not evil, and prosperity is not evil, either. It is the love of money that is evil.

> For the love of money is the root of all evil: which while some coveted after, they have erred from the faith, and pierced themselves through with many sorrows.
>
> 1 Timothy 6:10, *KJV*

## Money Is Simply A Tool... A Tool Used To Spread The Gospel!

I am in full agreement that money can be abused, and it certainly has been. But that does not mean God is against the pure form of it. In fact, God has given His people the power to get wealth for the purpose of establishing His Covenant.

> But thou shalt remember the LORD thy God: for it is he that giveth thee power to get wealth, that he may establish his covenant which he sware unto thy fathers, as it is this day.
>
> Deuteronomy 8:18, *KJV*

So, before you judge a book by its cover, take a moment and read it. Whether you agree or not, you may discover some things along the way that just may open the door to the future God has had waiting for you...

God's Happiest Moment Is When He Is Believed; His Greatest Dis-appointment Is When He Is Doubted.

Chapter 2

# $LAVES TO A STINGY GOD

Imagine for a moment that we are the sons and daughters of a very wealthy father, whose riches are so great that no one can even begin to estimate his net worth. Now, imagine that we choose to live as paupers, embracing the idea that our father, because he supposedly loves us, requires of us that we live as paupers; he does not want to bless us nor allow us to partake of his riches.

Certainly, you can see that I am attempting to make a point.

What would others believe and think about him? Would they have any desire to seek and to know him more? Or, would they question whether he truly loved us?

Some may say, "Oh, but God allows us to partake of His richness of grace, mercy and love." True, but why do we believe He excludes the means by which men live here on earth?

Much too often, God's children, by the way they live, how they feel, and what they believe (even if it doesn't line up with the truth of Scripture), declare to the world that God, their loving Father, does not want to bless them, but desires for them to live an impoverished life. Does that sound like One who loves us? Are we really to believe that God was willing to give Jesus, His only Son, yet is unwilling to allow us to partake of His material things, His wealth?

Certainly, nothing compares to Jesus and His sacrifice. I know where I would be without Jesus in my life. I am not attempting to downplay or even compare the two, but I do believe the question is valid.

**He that spared not his own Son, but delivered him up for us all, how shall he not with him also freely give us all things?**
**Romans 8:32, *KJV***

God is abundantly wealthy. Not just spiritually, but materially as well. No one can even begin to estimate His net worth. If we accumulated, into one spot, all the money of the wealthiest men on earth, it would not even be a speck in the vast universe of God's wealth.

**For every beast of the forest is mine, and the cattle upon a thousand hills.**
**Psalm 50:10, *KJV***

**The silver is mine, and the gold is mine, saith the LORD of hosts.**
**Haggai 2:8, *KJV***

Not only is God abundantly wealthy, but His name is *Jehovah-Jireh*, which means *One who abundantly provides for His children.*

And Abraham called the name of that place The LORD Will Provide, as it is said to this day, "In the mount of the LORD it will be provided."

Genesis 22:14, *NASB*

And my God will supply all your needs according to His riches in glory in Christ Jesus.

Philippians 4:19, *NASB*

## Whom Do We Serve?

In light of these realities, let's ask ourselves some elementary but very key questions:

- Are we presenting to the world that our God is generous or stingy, abundantly blessed or a greedy tyrant?

- Is our Heavenly Father *Jehovah-Jireh (the God who provides)* or simply Jehovah?

- Do we believe that God loves us and desires our prosperity?

Which God do you serve? A generous or stingy God? Perhaps it would be helpful to get more specific. Let's ask ourselves if we agree or disagree with the following statements:

- While the streets of Heaven are paved with gold, our Heavenly Father says gold and silver are not for us, in this life, here on this earth.

- While God's residence, Heaven, is decked out in splendor, our homes should be only humble huts.

- Life is simply a journey to get to Heaven, and none of Heaven's blessings or riches are available to us along the way.

- While we are on the journey to Heaven, in order to be truly pleasing to God, we must sacrifice the truly good things of this life every step of the way.

- We must watch our pennies, only for the purpose that we will have enough excess money to do our part in supporting God's plan for world evangelism.

- Each time we hear of a great need, we want to give, but we just never seem to have enough money to do it the way we really desire.

## Our Actions Mirror Our Beliefs

This is the reason no one set sail before Christopher Columbus. They believed the earth was flat. To set sail was suicidal. It's the same reason a young girl can be hospitalized and weight 75 lbs and still resist food because she believes she is overweight.

Think about this for a moment: In the Christian market, movies are produced to be a media vehicle for the gospel. When these movies are released, what do Christians pray for? They pray that the Christian movie will be successful, touching the lives it was intended to reach, but also, that it would bring in enough finances to be the seed for the next movie that's soon to be released. Most Christians seem to think that these prayers are perfectly acceptable. We willingly join our Christian brothers and sisters in asking God to bless the project, to make it successful, and to bring in the finances necessary to ensure its longevity. Yet, we find it very difficult to believe that God, in His basest, most foundational thought, has a will that we, His children, would live in financial abundance.

Again, financial "abundance" simply means this: *That you would have not only enough to meet your own needs, but also enough to help meet the needs of others.*

For each person, this definition will take on different characteristics. For example, financial prosperity for Tim might be $700 per month, enough to cover his $350 apartment rent, his utilities, and his car expenses, with some left over to spare. However, for Melanie, whose mortgage payment is $4000 per month, financial prosperity means something entirely different. You see, prosperity is subjective and ever moving. If you defined prosperity from *God's perspective*, how do you think it would look?

**Prosperity has more to do with your mind than with your pocketbook.** Prosperity has everything to do with your perspective, or the way you think. Not necessarily *what* you think, but rather, *the way* you think. Do you think God wants you to prosper, or do you think God wants you to be poor? Which *way* do you think? Whatever you believe becomes evident in your life. It is impossible to hide what you believe.

> Don't copy the behavior and customs of this world, but
> let God transform you into a new person by <u>changing the
> way you think</u>...
>
> Romans 12:2, *NLT* [emphasis added]

> And do not be conformed to this world, but be trans-
> formed by the renewing of your mind, that you may prove
> what is that good and acceptable and perfect will of God.
>
> **Romans 12:2**

We cannot even begin to know God's will for our prosperity *until* we renew our minds. Sadly, the customs and behaviors of this world include the *mammon system*, which we will ultimately follow *unless* we renew our minds with God's Word. I like to say it like this when it comes to our mind...

## Your Hair Stays Combed Longer Than Your Mind Stays Renewed.

People stubbornly hold on to beliefs that are most often formed by past experiences or by rigid doctrine that they have heard. After years of being allowed to go unchecked, these thoughts are formed into beliefs that govern, and ultimately control, the lives of those who adopt them.

We must understand that we are each a living prophecy of what we believe. If we believe that God wants us poor, or that poverty is our destiny, life proves that out for us. If we believe that God wants us blessed, life will also prove that to be true.

Now, before you put this book down because you think it's going to be "just another book about prosperity," please hear me out. I don't want anyone to think that a person can be prosperous simply because he quotes a few Scriptures and confesses that God wants him to be blessed. Many ministers on television will tell you that there's a miracle on its way and that you don't have to do anything for it. But friend, understand, that is not the way God works. God requires faith that results in action on our part. He has said in the Scriptures that if a man won't work, neither shall he eat.

> **For even when we were with you, we commanded you this: If anyone will not work, neither shall he eat.**
>
> **2 Thessalonians 3:10**

Just as there are Christians who think that poverty is a sign of godliness and nobility, there are those in the other ditch who think that God is somehow going to take the wealth of the diligent, hard-working non-believer and give it to a lazy believer who is just waiting for money to grow on trees. I can guarantee it's not going to happen that way either! So, I'd like to teach you about a process, the steps that you and I must take to become what God has called us to become and to stay that way.

# Prosperity Is Having More Than Enough Provision To Fulfill What God Requires.

Chapter 3

# IMPRI$ONED
# BY LACK

Before we receive Jesus Christ as Lord and Savior, we are all slaves to this way of life and the belief system called sin. The bondage of sin is brutal, and it is characterized by lives filled with despair, frustration, hopelessness, doubt, and worry. The harsh taskmaster of sin is ever ready to measure out punishment upon the slaves under his control. The wicked master of sinners demands complete obedience and allegiance, promising punishment to any who dare to disobey.

- Drug addicts who try to gain release from their addictions are instantly wracked with withdrawal pains.

- Embezzlers who want to confess and start over cannot because of the paralyzing fear that comes upon them.

- Abusers of other people are continually tortured by their own self-loathing.

- Deceived millions live under the unyielding pain and severity of being relentlessly stalked by poverty.

When the gospel of Jesus Christ illuminates our lives, we are set free from this evil slave master. In that one, marvelous instant, freedom becomes available to the newborn child of God! We no longer have to be subject to the oppression of Satan's kingdom. This is the good news that Jesus proclaims to the poor!

> **He has delivered us from the power of darkness and conveyed us into the kingdom of the Son of His love, in whom we have redemption through His blood, the forgiveness of sins.**
>
> Colossians 1:13-14

This is the good news that Jesus proclaims to the poor!

> **The Spirit of the LORD is upon Me, because He has anointed Me to preach the gospel to the poor...**
>
> Luke 4:18

Since Jesus bought and paid for our freedom with His precious blood, why is it that so many Christians continue to live in the bondage of lack and insufficiency? Why don't they come into the full liberty that God promises to all who receive Him?

Most of these wonderful people are still deceived and dominated by the same unseen influences that imprisoned them before they met the Lord. These uninformed Christians unwittingly continue to live the lifestyle that their former god demanded of them. While their eternal destiny has no doubt changed, they still live their present existence in the familiar clutches of lack. They are plagued with despair, hopelessness, poverty, and fear, continually suffering defeat and disappointment.

The harsh truth is that these defeated Christians have left one form of slavery only to enter into another. Unwittingly, they have been tricked into perceiving their new god as harsh and unfeeling toward them, a god who always demands and seldom gives. They serve their poorly funded churches as slaves, secretly dreading the next missions offering or building program. The unspoken question they are constantly asking themselves is, "How much will this cost?" These unfortunate saints are often impoverished and steeped in debt. They go from day to day without hope for anything much beyond their immediate needs. As they are asked to give, again and again, they can't help but wonder where it will come from this time.

## The Prison Door Is Open

It is interesting to observe the reaction of an animal that has been caged its entire life, when the door to its cage is opened. Most often, the creature will choose to remain in its cage. It feels most comfortable in the familiarity and predictability of its imprisoned surroundings, though the conditions are often meager and harsh. Long past and forgotten are the days of struggling against the binding chains in an attempt to find freedom. The unrelenting captivity has successfully trained the animal to remain a captive, even when given the opportunity to go free.

### You Are Either The Prisoner Of Your Past Or The Pioneer Of Your Future.

Sadly, many new believers unknowingly find themselves in a situation similar to the caged animal. The love of God has been shed abroad in their hearts (Romans 5:5, *KJV*); Jesus Christ has paid the price for their freedom and has opened their prison doors. However, because they have not yet renewed their minds to the freedom that is theirs (Romans 12:2), they continue to live in the familiar confines of financial bondage. The prison door may stand open; however, if a free man *perceives* (believes in his heart) that he is still a slave, then he will remain a slave.

## Whatever Controls Your Mind Controls Your Life.

This is why it is so important to renew our minds daily with Scriptures from "Heaven's Holy Writ." We must inundate our minds with divine thoughts, because it is only when we change the way we *think* that we will change the way we live.

# Your Projection Of God

Although perception will determine one's attitude, and therefore, one's reality, it is not necessarily factual. Just because you perceive something a certain way doesn't mean it really is that way. To see just how misleading your perception can be, consider the ancient Indian fable about six blind men trying to describe an elephant. The blind man who touched the elephant's leg said the elephant is like a pillar; the one who felt the tail said the elephant is like a rope; the man who felt the trunk said the elephant is like a tree branch; the one who felt the ear said the elephant is like a hand fan; the one who felt the belly said the elephant is like a wall; and the man who felt the tusk said the elephant is like a solid pipe. All of these perceptions were incorrect in defining a true composite picture of the elephant.

In the same way, if your perception of God comes from blind guides, your view of Him will be distorted.

> **...if the blind leads the blind, both will fall into a ditch.**
> **Matthew 15:14**

> **Blind guides, who strain out a gnat and swallow a camel!**
> **Matthew 23:24**

It is a fact that those who perceive and project God as poor must live with the consequences that come from serving a poor god. However, those who perceive and project God as He projects Himself will live with the abundant provisions of a rich God.

## All Significant Change Begins When You Make The Choice To Dismantle The Perceptions That Hinder You From Achieving Your Dreams.

It is also true that those who perceive God as one who desires them to barely get by will usually give their money only when there is a project that is designated as a *need*. This mentality causes them to give sacrificially to the church building fund, so that they can help provide the facility they believe their penniless god so desperately needs. However, once the structure is completed, they turn a deaf ear to the everyday, ongoing necessities, such as piano tuning or building upkeep. Because of their lack of sufficient surplus funds, they see insufficiency in everything they do. These slaves to the poor god are always trying to find cheaper ways of accomplishing things for their god. Whether or not they realize it, their lifestyles of constant insufficiency loudly proclaim to the world that their god is Jehovah-Needy, not Jehovah-Jireh!

Against popular opinion, let it be known to all that the God and Father of our Lord Jesus Christ is possessor of all riches – He is far from poor! He is sufficient, not needy. He gives abundantly to His children and does not grab everything He can from them. Know also, that He boldly proclaims His desire for His children to give liberally, so that He, the God of abundant provision, may liberally add to their wealth. This enables them to easily fund every joint effort God desires to undertake with them.

> ...God is able to make all grace abound toward you, that you, always having all sufficiency in all things, <u>may have an abundance for every good work</u>.
>
> **2 Corinthians 9:8 [emphasis added]**

## The Rich God Gives, The Poor God Takes

Your perception of God will determine how you relate to Him. People often perceive the character and purposes of God through the lens of negativity. Your perception of God determines your expectations of Him, good or bad. Change your perception, and your expectations will follow suit. Do you see God as a demanding taskmaster, uncaringly using all of your hard-earned money for His own glory, or do you see Him as someone who helps you get to the top? How do you see your financial challenges? Do you feel sad and frustrated that you don't have more money, or are you glad that your financial situation encourages you to plan your purchases wisely and guides you away from waste? Your perception makes all the difference.

There are always two ways to perceive everything, and the choice is always yours to make!

## Success And Failure Are Discretionary Destinations; Choices Are The Paths That Determine Them.

To understand this truth more clearly, let's examine the Parable of the Talents in the Book of Matthew. The steward with one talent *perceives* (believes in his heart) that his master is a harsh, greedy, and unjust man (Matthew 25:24-25). However, contrary to what the misguided, one-talent steward perceived, or thought he knew, the Bible plainly states that the master, in this parable, is a good and generous lord.

> For the kingdom of heaven is like a man traveling to a far country, who called his own servants <u>and delivered his goods to them</u>. And to one he gave five talents, to another two, and to another one, to each according to his own ability; and immediately he went on a journey.
>
> Matthew 25:14-15 [emphasis added]

Let's begin by allowing God's Word to establish the true nature of this master. Jesus tells us that he is a *giver*, not a taker. The Lord plainly states that the master *delivered his own goods to the servants.* He gave one servant five talents, another servant two, and another one. Nowhere does this parable state that the master wanted to take anything away from his servants.

The master in this parable is obviously representative of God the Father, the rich God who generously gives to His children, never desiring to take anything from them.

> **For the kingdom of heaven is like a man traveling to a far country, who called his own servants and delivered his goods to them.**
>
> Matthew 25:14

He is Jehovah-Jireh, the One who promises to provide substance and wealth to His children. Instead of grudgingly throwing five dollars at God's programs, the obedient children of God willingly *sow their financial seeds* into His good ground, desiring to promote His programs on the earth and expecting to truly experience the joy of the harvest that He promises.

> **Yes, God will give you much so that you can give away much...**
>
> 2 Corinthians 9:11, *TLB*

Be honest with yourself. *Do those around you perceive your God to be a giver or a taker?* Is He one who provides or one who impoverishes? One who demands provision from you or one who abundantly supplies provision to you and for you?

Notice, the master in this parable does not say, "Take your hard-earned wages and give them to me." Instead, the master *graciously gives his goods* to his servants, entrusting them with the privilege of handling his money. He trusts them to be his representatives. They know their master's desires and how he wants them to handle the money he has so graciously given them.

Let's examine the difference between the poor god and the rich God, and the difference between being a trusted steward or being little more than a slave.

- The poor god continually demands that his slaves give him an ever-increasing part of their meager goods; the rich God entrusts his stewards with an ever-increasing portion of his goods.

- The poor god distrusts his servants when it comes to money matters. This is obvious from the fact that he severely limits the amount of excess funds he allows them to have. The rich God continues to entrust his stewards with an ever-increasing amount of wealth and influence, as they prove themselves trustworthy in redistributing the things he places into their hands.

Are you beginning to get the picture? God wants to trust you. He wants to help you manage wealth in such a way that you will be able to bless all the families of the earth!

> **...you shall be a blessing. I will bless those who bless you, And I will curse him who curses you; And in you all the families of the earth shall be blessed.**
>
> **Genesis 12:2-3**

Let the following Scripture establish within you the wonderful truth that the God of Heaven is a generous giver.

> **For God so loved the world that He gave His only begotten Son...**
>
> John 3:16

It is an unchanging truth that the supreme, ultimate gift comes from the rich God, who unselfishly gave the world His best – His only Son, Jesus Christ!

The rich God of Heaven is on the record about His generosity in giving, for He declares that He has set aside each generous portion of this world's wealth for every human being on planet earth:

> **Here is what I have seen: It is good and fitting for one to eat and drink, and to enjoy the good of all his labor in which he toils under the sun all the days of his life which God gives him; for it is his heritage. As for every man to whom God has given riches and wealth, and given him power to eat of it, to receive his heritage and rejoice in his labor – this is the gift of God.**
>
> Ecclesiastes 5:18-19 [emphasis added]

Think about it. These verses boldly declare that the rich God of Heaven is a giver – not a taker – for He graciously promises, every day of your life, to give you:

- All you will ever need to eat and drink
- Full-time employment and joy in the fruit of your labor
- More than enough wealth and riches to accomplish His plan for your life

• An unending stream of joy in your heart

In other words, one of the rich God's top priorities is to give you the good life!

The Apostle John bears witness to this fact when he declares that his top prayer for all of God's children is that they prosper and be in good health.

> **Beloved, I pray that you may prosper in all things and be in health, just as your soul prospers.**
>
> **3 John 2**

Best of all, the Lord Jesus Himself backs this up when He declares His unselfish purpose for coming to earth:

> **...I have come that they may have <u>life</u>, and that they may have it <u>more abundantly</u>.**
>
> **John 10:10 [emphasis added]**

God
Will Never
Give You
A Future
That
Makes Him
Unnecessary.

Chapter 4

# GOD SHALL $UPPLY

One of the greatest truths about the rich God of Heaven is that He doesn't expect His children to supply His needs. Notice this truth in light of Scripture:

> **If I were hungry, I would not tell you; for the world is Mine, and all its fullness.**
>
> **Psalm 50:12**

The Apostle Paul writes the rest of this story when he tells us whose responsibility it is to do the supplying, in the relationship between God the Father and His children.

> **And my <u>God shall supply</u> all your need according to His riches in glory by Christ Jesus.**
>
> **Philippians 4:19 [emphasis added]**

Carefully notice that he doesn't say God's children will supply all of the Father's needs according to the abundance of their sweat and toil.

Scripture abounds with verses that loudly proclaim that God is a giver. It is His very nature to give. Therefore, if we are renewing our minds and allowing the Holy Spirit to recreate us into His image, we will find a new nature growing in us that will transform us into the same kind of givers as our Heavenly Father. However, if we have somehow been tricked into believing that our god is a taker, we will subconsciously begin to conform to this misconceived image of God. This misconception will cause us to steadily become takers instead of givers.

The children of God know, beyond any shadow of doubt, that their God is a *giver*, and because of this knowledge, they are also becoming givers.

## What Is Our Motivation?

Remember the truth of the Parable of the Talents: *We will have the god we perceive.* If we perceive God's program to be overrun with need, we will feel the necessity to give only where the need is the greatest.

Not only that, but our perception of God dictates how we manage our finances. If we perceive our god to be constantly in need, we will tend to be overly cautious, releasing no more of our meager assets than absolutely necessary. By contrast, those who perceive God as a giver know that it is only in giving, releasing, and sowing that one will ever be able to fully realize the true purpose for the abundance God has so richly promised to provide.

## We Will Always Move In The Direction Of Our Most Dominant Thoughts.

If fear causes us to focus on bills and debt, we will inadvertently move toward lack and poor financial decisions. If our focus is on a loving God, then our focus will be on love, because God is love (1 John 4:16), and on giving, because God is a giver (John 3:16).

> **And we have known and believed the love that God has for us. God is love, and he who abides in love abides in God, and God in him.**
>
> **1 John 4:16**

> **For God so loved the world that He gave His only begotten Son, that whoever believes in Him should not perish but have everlasting life.**
>
> **John 3:16**

> **There is no fear in love, but perfect love casts out fear, because fear involves torment. But he who fears has not been made perfect in love. We love Him because He first loved us.**
>
> **1 John 4:18-19**

We must always remember that the only way to overcome fear is to face it and cast it out. The giant named FEAR always seems more terrible than he really is. We will prevail if we run toward our giants and face them head on!

Let's again examine the perception of the one-talent steward:

> Then he who had received the one talent came and said, "Lord, I knew you to be a hard man, reaping where you have not sown, and gathering where you have not scattered seed. And I was afraid, and went and hid your talent in the ground. Look, there you have what is yours."
>
> Matthew 25:24-25

It is interesting to note that, in this verse, the Greek form of the word "knew" is *ginosko*, which is the experiential knowledge form of the verb. It can be translated as "perceived" (Bromiley, *Geoffrey W. Theological Dictionary of the New Testament*. Grand Rapids, MI: William B. Eerdmans Publishing Company, 1985. p.119ff).

In the New Testament, the verb *ginosko* frequently indicates a relationship between the person "knowing" and the object known; in this respect, what is "known or perceived" is of importance to the one who "knows" and is a significant factor in the establishment and nature of the relationship. Jesus confirms this relationship dynamic by telling how each steward's *perception* of his master directly affects the way he handles his master's goods.

> Then he who had received the five talents went and traded with them, and made another five talents. And likewise he who had received two gained two more also. But he who had received one went and dug in the ground, and hid his lord's money.
>
> Matthew 25:16-18

The first two servants correctly perceive their master to be a rich and trusting provider. Because of their perception, they prove to be faithful stewards of that which he gives them. They are confident their master is a good, generous, and loving lord. They perceive him to be a giver, not a taker. Out of love, they wisely use that which he entrusts to them to increase the kingdom of their benevolent lord.

However, the misinformed, one-talent servant perceives himself to be the slave of a hard, unjust, and self-serving master. Out of fear, this steward hides his lord's money. Understanding his master to be greedy, this slave selfishly holds on to everything he gets his hands on.

The poor slave never learned the divine truth that there can be no harvest unless something is sown. Neither can there be any increase until something is released! Fearfully guarding his meager little handful, the foolish slave hides his money, dreading the wrath of his master, whom he perceives to be harsh, unjust, and self-serving.

### For Every Seed We Sow, There Is A Proportionate Harvest; A Seed Of Nothing Produces A Season Of Nothing.

Consider, for a moment, the many things we desperately hold on to because of our fear of losing them. Yet, Jesus declares whoever will gain his life (his soul and the things pertaining to the natural realm) shall lose it, but whoever will lose his life, for Christ's sake, will gain life (Matthew 10:39). The amazing truth of all of this is that a real steward has absolutely nothing to lose, for everything placed under his control already belongs to God!

The misinformed servant never realized that the money his master placed in his hand was not his harvest; it was merely his seed!

> **For God...will give you more and more seed to plant...**
> **2 Corinthians 9:10, *TLB***

If we live our lives holding on to everything, we can be assured that one day, when we stand before the Master of our stewardship, we will be totally ashamed of the way we handled God's money.

> **It is possible to give away and become richer! It is also possible to hold on too tightly and lose everything. Yes, the liberal man shall be rich! By watering others, he waters himself.**
>
> **Proverbs 11:24-25, *TLB***

> **Therefore if you have not been faithful in the unrighteous mammon, who will commit to your trust the true riches?**
>
> **Luke 16:11**

Wouldn't it be wonderful if the church would just drop the destructive tradition of poverty and do what Jesus told us to do? Wealth and prosperity would break forth in the church like never before. The increase of wealth would be so large that even the heathen would have to declare that the rich God of Heaven is the source of that which we believe.

"...Try it! Let me prove it to you! Your crops will be large, for I will guard them from insects and plagues. Your grapes won't shrivel away before they ripen," says the Lord of Hosts. "And all nations will call you blessed, for you will be a land sparkling with happiness. These are the promises of the Lord of Hosts."

Malachi 3:10-12, TLB

Give, and it will be given to you. A good measure, pressed down, shaken together and running over, will be poured into your lap. For with the measure you use, it will be measured to you.

Luke 6:38, NIV

That's exactly what happened to the five-talent and two-talent stewards of the parable. With the same measure that they gave, their lord generously multiplied it back to them.

The first two stewards perceived their master to be a rich and generous giver. When he gave his money into their care, they immediately put it to work accomplishing his purposes. Here's the bottom line of their great success: *They simply imitated their master's generous nature.*

What motivated them to portray to those around them a giving, trustworthy nature? It was the fact that they perceived their lord as generous, caring, and trustworthy. They simply imitated their master. And what motivated the misinformed steward to desperately clutch at what little he had? He was simply imitating what he erroneously *perceived* to be his master's nature.

> Therefore be imitators of God [copy Him and follow His
> example], as well-beloved children [imitate their father].
>
> Ephesians 5:1, *AMP*

## Ignorance: Our Greatest Enemy

Contrary to popular belief, ignorance is not bliss. Ignorance is our greatest enemy in life. The faithless servant perished for lack of knowledge (Hosea 4:6). We simply cannot rise above our understanding, and our present circumstances reveal the level of understanding we possess.

> **My people are destroyed for lack of knowledge. Because
> you have rejected knowledge, I also will reject you from
> being priest for Me; Because you have forgotten the law of
> your God, I also will forget your children.**
>
> **Hosea 4:6**

All Bible believers know they are made in God's image and possess His basic nature. Therefore, if we see a Christian acting fearful, he no doubt perceives his God as fearful. However, when we see Christians who are generous, liberally giving into every good work, it is evident that they perceive their God as rich and generous. Their generous lifestyle openly declares to the world that they serve the rich God of the Bible. Read it from God's own Word.

> **Let your light so shine before men, that they may see
> your good works and glorify your Father in heaven.**
>
> **Matthew 5:16**

This verse clearly tells us to live our lives before men in such a good and generous way that they will see in us the love and generosity of God, causing them to glorify God.

We have had the privilege of being in the presence of our Heavenly Father since our new lives in Christ began. We have witnessed the extravagance of His creation. We know our Heavenly Father's goodness. If, for some reason, we have missed the truth that our good God is also a wealthy God who is pleased to see His children prosper, this error has, no doubt, come about by some mistaken religious tradition.

In the Book of Psalms, we find the following exhortation:

> **Let them shout for joy and be glad, Who favor my righteous cause; And let them say continually, "Let the LORD be magnified, Who has pleasure in the prosperity of His servant."**
>
> **Psalm 35:27**

David clearly stated the truth that God receives pleasure from the prosperity of those who are serving Him. The question is whether or not we are serving Him. I would like to believe that I am, and I pray that you are, just as well. Therefore, the Scripture stands true for us – *God has pleasure in our prosperity.*

The question becomes, "What, exactly, is prosperity?"

## Prosperity Is
## Having More Than Enough Assets
## To Complete Our Assignment.

The misinformed servant in Matthew 25 already had prosperity. His master had given him what he needed to complete his assignment. However, his response reflected fear, lack, and poverty thinking. He put his trust in the money he could see, instead of trusting in the unseen principles of faith, to bring the assignment to pass (Proverbs 11:28).

## Prosperity In Life
## Is In Direct Proportion To Our Willingness
## To Trust In The God Of The Bible.

**God is not a man, that He should lie, nor a son of man, that He should repent. Has He said, and will He not do? Or has He spoken, and will He not make it good?**

**Numbers 23:19**

**My covenant I will not break, nor alter the word that has gone out of My lips.**

**Psalm 89:34**

This servant did not realize that the measure of the seed one scatters determines the size of the harvest one reaps. Nor did he see God as a good God who desires to bless His children.

**The blessing of the LORD makes one rich, and He adds no sorrow with it.**

**Proverbs 10:22**

Moses instructed the people of Israel:

> And you shall remember the LORD your God, for it is He
> who gives you power to get wealth, that He may establish His
> covenant which He swore to your fathers, as it is this day.
>
> Deuteronomy 8:18

It is a divine truth that God responds in a positive way to each of His servants who properly use His money, saying, "Well done, good and faithful servant; you were faithful *over a few things,* I will make you ruler *over many things...*" (Matthew 25:21, 23 [emphasis added]).

Carefully notice that the master does not argue with the fearful servant, who mistakenly perceives his master to be hard and selfish. Neither does he try to correct his servant's misconception of him. Instead the master allows him to remain in his deception.

> ...you knew [perceived] that I reap where I have not
> sown, and gather where I have not scattered seed.
>
> Matthew 25:26

Here we see that God freely allows people to have the god they perceive!

## I Knew You Were A Hard Man

Notice how stubbornly the one-talent servant hangs on to the misconception of his master's true nature. He continues in error, even though everything the master had ever done for him was kind, loving, and generous. He continues to believe the lie that his master is a hard man.

37

Then the man with $1,000 came and said, "Sir, I knew you were a hard man, and I was afraid you would rob me of what I earned, so I hid your money in the earth and here it is!" But his master replied, "Wicked man! Lazy slave! Since you knew I would demand your profit, you should at least have put my money into the bank so I could have some interest. Take the money from this man and give it to the man with $10,000. For the man who uses well what he is given shall be given more, and he shall have abundance. But from the man who is unfaithful, even what little responsibility he has shall be taken from him. And throw the useless servant out into outer darkness: there shall be weeping and gnashing of teeth."

Matthew 25:25-30, TLB

What a person learns, experiences, and understands about something or someone shapes his perception of it. So, the wicked servant was actually saying, "Based on what I have been taught and what I understand about my master, I perceive him to be a taker, not a giver." Perception, even if it is based on erroneous information or on misunderstanding, will determine our concept of a situation or person. Then we will act based on those perceptions. The result is that our perception becomes our reality.

## Your Mind Is The Soil
## Where The Seeds of Perception
## Produce Consistent Actions.

The greater part of the traditional church carries a wrong perception of God, one that is based on the teachings of misled ministers who acquired their training in traditional religious institutions. These schools taught their students that God's many outreaches would be in constant need of financial support. This erroneous teaching has led entire denominations and religious organizations to the subconscious conclusion that God must be in some kind of need, or at best, suffering from a severe cash flow problem. This belief has caused certain denominations to dry up both spiritually and financially. As they believe their own press releases regarding their financial need, they create a self-fulfilling prophecy. When this occurs, they do not even realize what has happened.

We must be careful not to base any of our beliefs about God's desire for our financial status on the perceptions of man. We must carefully base every concept we form about God's attitude toward us, and our well-being, firmly on "thus saith the Word of the Lord." Only the truth of God's Word can set a person free from the *mistaken* perception that God continually runs His business in some form of financial shortfall.

A person's mind is never neutral – it is always believing *something!* And as we discussed earlier, whatever controls one's mind controls the outcome of his life. At this very moment, each one of us is operating either in mind prosperity or in a poverty mentality. If we want to change our lives, we will first have to change our minds.

### The Transformation Of One's Life Is In Direct Proportion To The Willingness to Change One's Mind.

For to be carnally minded is death, but to be spiritually minded is life and peace. Because the carnal mind is enmity against God; for it is not subject to the law of God, nor indeed can be. So then those who are in the flesh cannot please God.

**Romans 8:6-8**

I have learned in life that the "mind" was neither good nor bad. It functioned by its many influences. Our minds are a sponge awaiting the information we willingly exposed them to or the information that was unwillingly infused within us. Our actions were a reflection of that which momentarily controlled our mind, thus as a function of the mind.

The human life can be altered as well as engineered by the commitment to occupying one's mind with that which will build oneself up and not continue to be one's "own worst enemy".

Our perceptions and corresponding attitudes are magnetic, either attracting or repelling the lives we desire. Our perception of God directly affects our finances. Why? Because our future is built or destroyed by the relationships we embrace. Is our relationship with a rich God or a poor god?

## Misguided Giving

One of the traditional teachings in the church is sacrificial giving. It teaches that an individual must periodically sacrifice – do without, cut back, and limit himself – so that he will have something extra special to give to God. This erroneous thought process is in full swing in the traditional church of our day. It becomes evident as we hear the professional fundraisers using the following slogan to promote considerable giving to today's super-expensive building programs: "Not equal giving but equal sacrifice."

Thousands of well-meaning believers give in this way. Yes, they give in faith. However, it is not the kind of faith that is believing for an abundant increase. They give in faith, believing that if they tighten up their budget and spend less money, then they are preparing to give. Please pay close attention. This is not the kind of faith that brings a financial harvest. It is nothing more than faith to be able to get by on what is leftover, instead of true biblical faith to believe for the harvest-proportion increase that God has promised.

We must understand that the type of faith we exert toward any desired result becomes the raw material that God will use to produce the thing we have asked for.

> **Now faith is the substance [raw material] of things hoped for, the evidence of things not seen.**
>
> **Hebrews 11:1**

Because of this biblical truth, it is of the utmost importance that we give with the kind of faith that believes we will receive a multiplied increase of that which we are giving. If we give with faith that believes we will be able to get by on less, the faith we use will bring forth the frugal lifestyle that we need for getting by on less. However, that particular kind of faith (or raw material) cannot bring forth a financial harvest of thirty, sixty, or hundredfold increase. In the same way that the raw material of cotton fibers cannot bring forth a steel beam, so the raw material of getting by on less than before cannot bring forth a harvest of having more than before.

A well-intentioned person might say, "I would like to tithe ninety percent of my income." Now, in itself, that's a noble thought. It comes from a person who desires to do a good work by tightening up the budget and suffering for Jesus. However, it is also an uninformed thought, for in Christ Jesus, there is a promise of much more than that.

Conversely, a person with a higher level of understanding of the full potential that exists in Christ Jesus might say, "I am going to believe God that my tithe will soon become more than the amount that I am now earning." This statement comes from the person who has faith to believe God for a harvest-proportion increase and the abundance God has promised.

There is, however, a type of sacrificial giving that pleases God. This kind of giving is not the kind that exercises faith to "get by on less," but rather, the type that has faith in, and is motivated by, the extravagance of God's love.

> **...faith activated and energized and expressed and working through love.**
>
> **Galatians 5:6, *AMP***

In fact, this type of giver is so confident in love's inability to fail (1 Corinthians 13:8), that he willingly, gratefully, and cheerfully sacrifices his own short-term pleasure to expedite the long-term freedom and deliverance of another. When we give this way, we are imitating our Heavenly Father, who sacrificially gave His Son for our salvation. Our motivation for giving must always have one focus: *To be an instrument of blessing to others.*

There are some believers who are experiencing this kind of potential. It is not that they are living on less, for they are actually living on exceedingly, abundantly more than they could have ever asked or thought (Ephesians 3:20). They now have more to give than they could have imagined possible just a few years ago. They have experienced this increase by faithfully operating the principle of seedtime and harvest in every area of their lives. They have done this by moving to a new kind of faith. It is not faith for decreased living expenses, but a much higher faith that is activated, energized, expressed, and working through love. It moves them to significantly increase their sowing into God's kingdom, believing that they will bring freedom and deliverance to others, and also believing that they will experience a thirty, sixty, or even hundredfold increase from their giving.

However, all too many of our Lord's precious children are enslaved by the church's teaching about a needy god. In spite of this, there is good news on the horizon. All of this mistaken theology is about to change, for God's Word promises that, as the coming of the Lord draws near, a great wave of correction will sweep across the church.

> **Whom heaven must receive [and retain] until the time for the complete restoration of all that God spoke by the mouth of all His holy prophets for ages past [from the most ancient time in the memory of man].**
>
> **Acts 3:21,** *AMP*

The Bible tells us that the time has come for God's ultimate desire for His children to come to pass. A great end-time restoration is about to break out across the church of God. A careful reading of Acts 3:19-21 will show us a promise from God, through the Apostle Peter. It is a prophecy, and it declares that all the errors of organized religious doctrine will be put straight, before Jesus returns. Yes, Simon Peter was saying exactly what it sounds like...

Restoration is coming and is at work even now!

# Money Is The Vehicle By Which God Finances Bringing The World To Himself.

Chapter 5

# THE ORIGIN OF THE POVERTY DOCTRINE

Many people believe poverty and prosperity are both matters of birth or luck. They believe some people are meant to be poor and others are meant to be rich. Others, especially a portion of Christians, honestly believe poverty is godly. They think that if a Christian is poor, he must be in the center of God's will. Some misguided groups of people even believe that by taking vows of poverty, they will somehow be more godly or more believable to those who hear them share the gospel.

To properly understand the origin of the poverty doctrine, one must be aware of the fact that the doctrinal mindset of the traditional church is founded on a pre-Reformation mentality. This included the belief that if riches for the believer were delayed until the hereafter, it would be a great motivator to keep people in proper relationship with God and the church. Very sadly, I admit that this has some truth to it.

However, it only stands to reason that when the world sees the impoverished slaves of this misguided system, they will have to believe that these Christians serve a poor god, or at best, a

47

selfish god who offers nothing more than a religion tailor-made for poor people. That's why it has been said that Christianity is a poor man's religion. Ted Turner even said, "Christianity is a religion for losers."

God has established certain principles of economics that govern prosperity and poverty, and He will not violate His own laws. If we follow and focus on the principles that lead to poverty, we will be poor. If we follow and focus on the principles that lead to prosperity, we will be anything but. We each play an important part in determining our own financial situations.

## What We Focus On Will Continue To Grow.

Satan plays his part, too. He will lie to us in every imaginable way to keep us poor, often using the religious traditions of men to deliver his lies. He will tell us myths about money. He will say that money is evil or that money will corrupt us. He will suggest that it is godly to be poor or that we will become even poorer if we give to God.

You see, poverty is a partnership. The devil wants us to be poor, and he will lie to us to keep us from following the biblical principles that will result in wealth. Poverty is a joint venture between us, Satan, and our ignorance of God's Word.

# Our Spiritual Family Tree

These myths and misconceptions must be exposed and re-jected, for the church's biblical heritage in no way supports the doctrine or the lifestyle of poverty. The Bible declares that Christianity finds its spiritual roots in a very rich man, for our earliest patriarch, Abraham, was extremely rich.

**Abram was very rich in livestock, in silver, and in gold.**
**Genesis 13:2**

Not only was Abraham rich, but Adam (the original father of the human race) was also rich. Adam was, without a doubt, the richest man that ever lived. He was so rich that he actually had legal control of every asset on the planet.

**Then God blessed them, and God said to them, "Be fruit-ful and multiply; fill the earth and subdue it; have dominion over the fish of the sea, over the birds of the air, and over every living thing that moves on the earth." And God said, "See, I have given you every herb that yields seed which is on the face of all the earth, and every tree whose fruit yields seed; to you it shall be for food."**
**Genesis 1:28-29**

Upon further examination of our spiritual family tree, we will find that, down through the ages, a great number of God's people were wealthy. For example, Job was exceedingly wealthy. Not only that, but when God restored him, He did not deplete his wealth; He actually doubled it. Interestingly enough, if God had wanted

Job to be poor, He could have simply healed him of his festering boils and left him in poverty. But that is not what God did.

> **And the LORD restored Job's losses when he prayed for his friends. Indeed the LORD gave Job twice as much as he had before.**
>
> Job 42:10

Isaac is also credited with having a tremendous amount of wealth. His riches were greatly increased by his sowing and reaping. The Bible says he became so rich, through the harvest he reaped, that the Philistines envied him.

> **Isaac planted crops in that land and the same year reaped a hundredfold, because the LORD blessed him. The man became rich, and his wealth continued to grow until he became very wealthy. He had so many flocks and herds and servants that the Philistines envied him.**
>
> Genesis 26:12-14, *NIV*

The patriarch Jacob also abounded with great wealth. The biblical record tells us that he "increased exceedingly".

> **Thus the man became exceedingly prosperous, and had large flocks, female and male servants, and camels and donkeys.**
>
> Genesis 30:43, *KJV*

While the Scriptures do not give us any details about the personal wealth of Joseph, they do describe his great power and influence in the financial and governmental affairs of Egypt, which was the superpower of his day (Genesis 41).

Each one of these men increased in wealth by understanding and operating the law of sowing and reaping. The heart of prosperity is revealed in the heart of a sower. One will never find the heart of prosperity in the life of a hoarder.

### Poverty Is Not The Lack Of Money; Poverty Is The Proof Of Misguided Money.

In an open-minded and fully informed investigation into the personal wealth of the forefathers of the Judeo-Christian faith, the evidence is overwhelming. The poverty doctrine did not come into the church through any facts from the biblical record. It had to creep in some other way – that way being the craftiness of the devil and the erroneous doctrines of men.

## Are We Enslaved To Jehovah-Needy?

As we consider these thought-provoking ideas, some of us may, even now, be realizing that we have somehow become trapped in a deadly misperception. In fact, we might be realizing that we are among those who provide living proof to the world that our god is Jehovah-Needy. We need to ask ourselves a very important question, one that has the potential of turning everything around for us and our loved ones: *Would we be willing to change something we believe, even if it went against everything we had previously been taught?*

Here's the Bible answer to that question:

> **...let God be true but every man a liar...**
>
> **Romans 3:4**

We may find ourselves in the same situation as the one-talent servant of our parable. We may be serving the poor god. We might not even know that we stand in danger of missing out on most of the good things God has planned for us.

> **So take the talent from him, and give it to him who has ten talents.**
>
> **Matthew 25:28**

Some of us might be asking, "How did this happen to me?" The answer is simple. We have unwittingly been led into the *rut of the poverty doctrine*. This misconception comes by the false theology of those who serve the poor and needy god, the god who demands that his subjects dutifully fund the projects he so desperately needs. And if that weren't enough, this same poor god also expects his followers to bail him out of every financial jam he gets into. Here's the truth that cannot be denied:

• **People serving a poor god raise money for him and his projects.** The poor god is the god of the world's *religious* system. He insists that his servants eke out a meager existence, for themselves and for his church, from the crumbs that fall from the lavishly supplied table of this world's system. They are forced to live with meager resources while being constantly plundered by their self-serving god. They mistakenly believe that this world's flawed financial system is dominant over the financial system of

God's kingdom. They are desperately trying to fund the kingdom of their god out of the dregs that the world leaves for them.

• **The poor god has poor slaves.** The poor god's system of sanctification demands that those who want to be truly spiritual must remain poor. They must operate their lives and ministries on the premise of meeting only the most urgent need. They must constantly struggle to acquire that which their religion needs instead of qualifying for God's plan of stewardship that brings exceedingly, abundantly more than they can ask.

> **Now to Him who is able to do exceedingly abundantly above all that we ask or think, according to the power that works in us,**
>
> **Ephesians 3:20**

• **Those who believe in the poor god have made an indictment against God.** They presuppose that He is a negligent Father who does not care for His own children.

> **But if anyone does not provide for his own, and especially for those of his household, he has denied the faith and is worse than an unbeliever.**
>
> **1 Timothy 5:8**

Once again, it becomes obvious that this mistaken, ragtag band of saints causes the world to conclude that their poor god most definitely needs a name change from Jehovah-Jireh to Jehovah-Needy.

## The God We Perceive

By now, the alarm bells of good sense should be ringing. Remember that the master in the Parable of the Talents allowed his servants the freedom to perceive him as they wished.

> **Then the man who had received the one talent came. "Master," he said, "I knew that you are a hard man, harvesting where you have not sown and gathering where you have not scattered seed. So I was afraid and went out and hid your talent in the ground. See, here is what belongs to you." His master replied, "You wicked, lazy servant! So you knew that I harvest where I have not sown and gather where I have not scattered seed? Well then, you should have put my money on deposit with the bankers, so that when I returned I would have received it back with interest."**
>
> **Matthew 25:24-27, *NIV***

With his completely wrong perception, the mistaken servant proved he had learned nothing about his master, even after serving him for years. In his flawed reasoning, he did not perceive his master's real nature; neither did he discern the true heart of his master. Because of his mistaken opinion, he could not project his master's real nature to the world. This fatal error in perception hopelessly locked him into becoming like Satan instead of like God, for Satan is the ultimate taker of all takers. Tragically, his inability to properly perceive his master's true nature led this servant into a wrong mentality that caused him to hide his master's money instead of using it in the way his master had intended.

# A Wise Servant Ensures That His Perception Is Defined By God And Not People.

As we continue examining these concepts, we will discover an ongoing stream of proofs from God's Word that will give us an undistorted biblical perception of the Almighty God of Heaven. From this information, we will become convinced that Jehovah God is the rich God who abundantly gave to Adam, Noah, Abraham, Isaac, Jacob, and Joseph. This same rich God also gave staggering amounts of tangible wealth to David and Solomon. He gave incalculable wealth to His Son, Jesus Christ, who stands ready to give to us in such a way that we will want for nothing.

> ...we went through fire and through water: but thou broughtest us out into a wealthy place.
>
> **Psalm 66:12, *KJV***

Remember these truths:

- The impoverished god of organized religion is Jehovah-Needy. He is the god whose servants must provide for him. The generous God of the Bible is Jehovah-Jireh, the God that provides for His children!

- The misguided slaves of a impoverished god raise money to fund his projects. The generous God of Heaven pours out abundant blessings upon His children, who join Him as co-laborers, making His kingdom on the earth, as it is in Heaven.

- The impoverished god needs slaves to gather up money for him. The generous God releases money to His children, so that they can redistribute it for His kingdom.

As stewards of the Most High God, you and I are one hundred percent responsible for how we respond to our Master's financial principles. It has become quite evident, hasn't it, that every principle, every perception, and every decision contains a predetermined outcome? The outcome of each of our lives is based solely upon the choices we make. Will we serve the impoverished, greedy god, or will we become a joint heir and co-laborer with the *generous* God?

## The Moment We Make A Decision Is The Moment We Have Determined Our Success Or Failure.

It's time for us to start believing God's Word instead of our traditional ideas. *God's Word does not teach poverty!* Let's choose *this day* to free ourselves from the poverty doctrine of this world's religious systems. We can become the privileged sons and daughters of the true and living God, who abundantly blesses His children with wealth so that they can be a blessing.

> ...I have set before you life and death, blessing and cursing; therefore choose life that both you and your descendants may live.
>
> **Deuteronomy 30:19**

Having established that the God of Heaven is the *rich* God, we can now turn our attention to another truth. The *generous God* freely gives us *His rich Son* to save us and help us obtain the abundant life He has purchased for us.

Prosperity Is Revealed To The Heart Of A Sower; You'll Never Find It In The Life Of A Hoarder.

# Chapter 6

# RICH JESU$: MYTH OR FACT?

Out of the greatest love ever known, God gave his Son to save, heal, deliver, and restore lost humanity. Everything the first Adam lost and brought to poverty, the second Adam (Jesus) redeemed and is now restoring to the total fullness God promised.

Asserting that Jehovah God is a rich God upsets almost no one. The truth is simply this: God is rich, and every thinking person believes that He should be.

> **...the earth is full of thy riches.**
>
> **Psalm 104:24,** *KJV*

Let me take a moment to give you just a partial list of Jehovah God's immeasurable wealth.

- **God's throne sits in a lavish setting of splendor and fine jewels.** *"And He who sat there was like a jasper and a sardius stone in appearance; and there was a rainbow around the throne, in appearance like an emerald" (Revelation 4:3).*

- **God possesses the greatest collection of the purest crystal in the universe.** *"Before the throne there was a sea of glass, like crystal..." (Revelation 4:6).*

- **The city of God is built of the purest of gold.** *"The construction of its wall was of jasper; and the city was pure gold..." (Revelation 21:18).*

- **The gates of God's city are made of solid pearl.** *"The twelve gates were twelve pearls: each individual gate was of one pearl..." (Revelation 21:21).*

- **The streets of His city are made of transparent gold.** *"...And the street of the city was pure gold, like transparent glass" (Revelation 21:21).*

- **God has an immeasurable inventory of possessions, including the cattle on a thousand hills, the whole earth, and all of its silver and gold** *(Psalm 50:10; 24:1, and Haggai 2:8).*

- **God is the sole owner of the entire universe and all it contains.** *"...He appointed [Jesus] Heir and lawful Owner of all things...upholding and maintaining and guiding and propelling the universe..." (Hebrews 1:2-3, AMP).*

Now, let me make ask a simple question:

*Would a rich Father insist that His obedient Son live in poverty?*

The answer would have to be a resounding NO!

At this very moment, in the midst of the Father's infinite riches, you will find His Son, Jesus Christ, reigning with Him.

In many separate revelations [each of which set forth a
portion of the Truth] and in different ways God spoke of old
to [our] forefathers in and by the prophets. [But] in the last
of these days He has spoken to us in [the person of a] Son,
Whom He appointed Heir and lawful Owner of all things,
also by and through Whom He created the worlds and the
reaches of space and the ages of time [He made, produced,
built, operated, and arranged them in order]. He is the sole
expression of the glory of God [the Light-being, the out-ray-
ing or radiance of the divine], and He is the perfect imprint
and very image of [God's] nature, upholding and maintaining and guiding and propelling the universe by His mighty
word of power. When He had by offering Himself accom-
plished our cleansing of sins and riddance of guilt, He sat
down at the right hand of the divine Majesty on high.

Hebrews 1:1-3, *AMP*

## The Substance Of Jesus' Family

And it came to pass in those days that a decree went
out from Caesar Augustus that all the world should be registered. This census first took place while Quirinius was
governing Syria. So all went to be registered, everyone to his
own city. Joseph also went up from Galilee, out of the city of
Nazareth, into Judea, to the city of David, which is called
Bethlehem, because he was of the house and lineage of
David, to be registered with Mary, his betrothed wife, who
was with child. So it was, that while they were there, the days

were completed for her to be delivered. And she brought forth her firstborn Son, and wrapped Him in swaddling cloths, and laid Him in a manger, because there was no room for them in the inn.

Luke 2:1-7

In their book, *Jesus and Wealth*, Dr. Peter and Graham J. Daniels noted the following:

> *One definition of wealth is "the ability to obtain what is immediately required, no matter what that need may be." Jesus was able to obtain what was immediately needed: a coin from the mouth of a fish, wine for a wedding, bread for a multitude, sight for the blind; He was beyond wealth. We must entertain the idea that there could possibly exist a level of wealth beyond our traditional definitions, and this level of wealth has been demonstrated by the man Jesus... [for example] researchers have demonstrated that the gifts of the Magi were not as our Christmas cards depict, but rather that their value could have been in excess of U.S. $400 million.*

(Excerpt from Jesus and Wealth,<br>by Dr. Peter and Graham J. Daniels)

Jesus was not born into a poor family! *Joseph's family had social standing, material wealth, and a solid business.* Let's not forget that Joseph was summoned to Bethlehem to be taxed. This would not be required of those who lived in poverty. Not only that, but Joseph was not looking for a barn in which to spend the night of our Lord's birth. Neither was he looking for a handout on his visit to Bethlehem. His plan was to rent a room at the inn. It is a well-established fact that the poor people of Israel, in those days, did not rent rooms in the local hotel. Paying for a room at the inn, when traveling, was costly. It was the practice of wealthy citizens to acquire paid lodging during times of travel.

Furthermore, the poor people of Joseph's time traveled on foot. Contrary to this, Joseph provided state-of-the-art transportation for his young wife; she rode on a donkey. In addition, the Bible also tells us that, after leaving Bethlehem, Joseph had sufficient money to finance a trip to Egypt that lasted until the death of Herod. After their extended stay in Egypt, Joseph had enough finances to transport Jesus and Mary back to Nazareth.

Also consider Jewish tradition, which dictated that the oldest son receive a double portion of his father's estate as his inheritance (Deuteronomy 21:17). Since we hear nothing about Joseph after the story of Jesus in the Temple at age twelve, most scholars believe, and I believe it is fair to say, that Joseph died before our Lord's public ministry began. This being the case, Jesus would have received the older son's double portion of His father's estate.

You must also keep in mind that Joseph wasn't just some no-name commoner who wandered about in Palestine. He was a direct descendant of the royal lineage of King David. That means He probably had some degree of social status. The Word of God tells us that Joseph was a carpenter by trade: "Is this not the carpenter's son? Is not His mother called Mary? And His brothers James, Joses, Simon, and Judas?" (Matthew 13:55).

The Greek construction in this verse implies that Joseph was very well-known in Nazareth – he was a famous citizen in this small community.

The fact is, Joseph was NOT a small-time carpenter; he was a MAJOR BUILDER, recognized for his profession and as a leader of the community. Joseph was one of the chief builders for the great city of Sepphoris.

What do we know about the city of Sepphoris, A city only 2.5 kilometers from Nazareth? Sepphoris, the capital of Galilee, was a MAJOR CITY built during the life of Jesus. Josephus, a first-century Jewish historian, called it the "Ornament of Galilee."

The largest part of Sepphoris was built while Joseph and Jesus were working together in the construction business, during Jesus' younger years. Because there was no construction work in Nazareth, there is no doubt that their primary building work was in the city of Sepphoris.

**The city of Sepphoris, located 2.5 kilometers from Nazareth, was:**

- The administrative city for Herod Antipas
- The biggest banking center of the region
- The greatest cultural city of the region, with the largest theater in the entire first-century world (more than 4,000 seats)
- A theater city, with famous actors, actresses, and other performers living and performing there on a regular basis
- "A city set on a hill" as Jesus described in the Sermon on the Mount (Matthew 5:14)

- Archeological excavations show that it was a very sophisticated city.

This means Jesus did not grow up in a poverty-stricken, uncultured village. As a young man, He was exposed to fine taste, culture, and lots of money. His earthly father was influential, prosperous, and recognized as a leader in the sleeper town of Nazareth. Growing up near Sepphoris exposed Jesus to all kinds of life.

Contrary to the picture people have in their minds of Jesus growing up in a poor, uncultured, impoverished community, Jesus grew up in an environment of education, culture and money.

As I said, the city of Sepphoris was just 2.5 kilometers from Nazareth. It had 30,000 residents, and it was an international city of Jews, Arabs, Greeks and Romans. It was linked to other major cities on the trade routes of the Greek-speaking world. Recent archeological digs prove that in Jesus' lifetime, Sepphoris was a <u>thriving metropolis</u>.

Even today, if you walk just ten minutes to the north of Nazareth, you will come to the top of a hill that gives you a clear view of this famous city of Sepphoris. It was literally a city that was "set on a hill" – probably the very picture Jesus had in His mind when He said: "A city that is set on a hill cannot be hidden" (Matthew 5:14).

Sepphoris was the capital of Galilee. As I said, it was the administrative headquarters of Herod Antipas, which explains why this particular Herod had heard so much of Jesus and had always wanted to meet Him.

> And when Herod saw Jesus, he was exceeding glad: for
> he was desirous to see him of a long season, because he had
> heard many things of him...
>
> **Luke 23:8, *KJV***

It makes sense that Herod Antipas had heard "many things" of Him, for Jesus and His foster father Joseph worked in the construction business to help build the city of Sepphoris.

What does the Bible mean when it says Joseph was a carpenter? When we think of a carpenter, we think of: Someone who works with wood and one who uses a hammer, saw, and nails. But in that world, a carpenter was:

- Someone who was a builder

- Someone who was an architect

- Someone who worked with stones and stone structures

- Someone who designed roads, buildings, and even furniture

- Someone who was very trained and skilled

In Matthew 13:55 and Mark 6:3, the Bible tells us that Joseph was a carpenter, the Greek word *tekton*, and again, it referred to a person who worked in the building business. It is so broad that it could refer to stone-building, wood-building, furniture-building – everything connected to building – including exquisite floors with inlaid stones or furniture inlaid with ivory. It could even be used to describe someone so skilled that he was capable of creating fine jewelry.

"Is this not the carpenter's son? Is not His mother called Mary? And His brothers James, Joses, Simon, and Judas?" (Matthew 13:55).

Matthew 13:55 indicates that Joseph was the most well-known "carpenter" who lived in Nazareth. Everyone in Nazareth knew him, Mary, and all the kids in the home. Because of the great skill needed to build the fabulous nearby city of Sepphoris, those who possessed these skills were highly paid. Joseph was well-known in the construction business; he was very established in it; and because of these things, he was recognized in the community.

It is also a well-founded belief that Joseph was a man of great integrity (Matthew 1:19). Therefore, as our Lord's earthly father, he would have projected a clear image of our Heavenly Father's nature to his children. Being a good man, chosen by God, Joseph would surely have established a good biblical heritage for his children – one that would have been in accordance with the instruction and expectation of God.

**A good man leaves an inheritance to his children's children...**

Proverbs 13:22

In fact, Joseph, as a proper earthly father, would undoubtedly have given a proper example of his rich Heavenly Father's love to his children. These are but a few of the undeniable proofs that Jesus did not grow up in a poverty-ridden family. There is no biblical proof that Joseph was a poor man.

## Jesus Wasn't Homeless

Another false assumption made by traditional religious teachers and their followers is that Jesus was homeless. This erroneous superstition is primarily based on a misunderstanding of something Jesus said as He passed through Samaria on His way to Jerusalem.

> **And Jesus said to him, "Foxes have holes and birds of the air have nests, but the Son of Man has nowhere to lay His head."**
>
> **Matthew 8:20**

It is interesting to note that in the context of this portion of Scripture, Jesus was not declaring that He was a vagabond. He clearly states in another portion of Scripture that He had an adequate home where He resided when He wasn't traveling. In the Gospel of John, Jesus openly declared that He had a home.

> **And the two disciples heard him speak, and they followed Jesus. Then Jesus turned, and saw them following, and saith unto them, What seek ye? They said unto him, Rabbi, (which is to say, being interpreted, Master,) where dwellest thou? He saith unto them, Come and see. They came and saw where he dwelt, and abode with him that day: for it was about the tenth hour.**
>
> **John 1:37-39, *KJV***

It is to the shame of organized religion that so many of the precious children of God are living with a mistaken perception of the financial status of the Son of God. This is a major doctrinal error that finds its roots in a total misunderstanding of Matthew 8:20 and Luke 9:58.

> ...Jesus said to him, "Foxes have holes and birds of the air have nests, but the Son of Man has nowhere to lay His head."
>
> Luke 9:58

From this isolated part of a much larger discourse, the religionists fabricate the false doctrine that Jesus must have been a homeless person. Now, I must confess that, outside of its proper context, it does sound as if He were declaring Himself to be homeless. However, when the exact context of our Lord's statement is taken into consideration, it establishes, without question, that was not what our Lord was saying.

Let's look at this story in its accurate context: Jesus sent an advance ministry team into Samaria to prepare a place for Him and His ministry staff to stay that night. However, Jesus and His disciples were rejected by the inhabitants of Samaria and were not allowed to enter the city.

> Now it came to pass, when the time had come for Him to be received up, that He steadfastly set His face to go to Jerusalem, and sent messengers before His face. And as they went, they entered a village of the Samaritans, to prepare for Him. But they did not receive Him, because His face was set for the journey to Jerusalem.
>
> Luke 9:51-53

The reason Jesus made the statement that He had no place to lay His head was not because He was poor and homeless; it was because *the Samaritans would not allow Him to remain in their city that night.*

## Jesus Dressed Well

While it is not central to the gospel account, the Scriptures nevertheless state that the clothing of our Lord was comparable to what we would call "nice apparel" in our day. This becomes apparent when we observe that, at Jesus' crucifixion, the Roman soldiers immediately recognized the value of his tailor-made coat and refused to divide it into pieces. Instead they decided to gamble to see who would be the new owner of this choice garment.

> Then the soldiers, when they had crucified Jesus, took His garments and made four parts, to each soldier a part, and also the tunic. Now the tunic was without seam, woven from the top in one piece. They said therefore among themselves, "Let us not tear it, but cast lots for it, whose it shall be…"
>
> John 19:23-24

Let me take a brief moment to answer yet another of the poverty proponents' foolish assertions about the expensive garment Jesus was wearing. Some people mistakenly allege, without any biblical foundation, that this splendid garment didn't actually belong to our Lord. They surmise that such a fine coat could not possibly be the property of the lowly Jesus. Therefore, they render a wild guess that some sympathetic rich person threw his coat over Jesus to cover His naked body, as He labored under the load of the cross on His way to Calvary. Not only is this conjecture without scriptural basis the Word of God absolutely refutes it, for the Bible states that this valuable garment was Jesus' own personal property.

"Let's not tear it," they said to one another. "Let's decide by lot who will get it." This happened that the scripture might be fulfilled which said, "They divided <u>my</u> garments among them and cast lots for <u>my</u> clothing."

John 19:24, *NIV* [emphasis added]

It quickly becomes evident to those who demand accurate biblical teaching that Jesus would have been a well-dressed man, for He was here on earth as the chief representative of His Father's rich kingdom. He was the most royal of all royal ambassadors that would ever be sent forth from the throne of God.

As the most distinguished representative to visit earth from Heaven, Jesus had everything He needed (including the appropriate attire) to properly operate His ministry, for His royal position included feeding, healing, and saving thousands at a time. Jesus also had a staff of disciples (at times, over seventy of them) who had specific responsibilities for making arrangements for the ministry's travel, lodging, food, and provisions.

# A Well-Financed Ministry

While on the earth, Jesus operated a large ministry with a substantial ministry team – one that needed sufficient funds to meet expenses, including feeding thousands of people when necessary. As we have already seen, Jesus had adequate funds to send out advance teams of ministries to arrange for His meetings and the housing of His staff. This is clear, from Scripture, when you read about His first recorded ministry visit to Samaria. He knew that He might not be a welcome guest.

> **...For Jews have no dealings with Samaritans.**
>
> John 4:9

Notice that the Bible says Jesus sent an advance team of disciples into the city to buy food.

> **For His disciples had gone away into the city to buy food.**
>
> John 4:8

Also, Jesus had a treasurer (Judas). Any thinking person knows there is no need for a treasurer unless there are significant enough funds to require a manager. In fact, our Lord's ministry had such an abundance of funds flowing into it that even with a treasurer who regularly stole from the account, there still remained a sufficient financial surplus to keep things operating in good order. The Bible tells us that Judas was regularly stealing funds from the treasury.

> **...he [Judas] was a thief, and had the money box; and he used to take what was put in it.**
>
> John 12:6

Once more, outstanding truth about Jesus and His financial ethics is revealed to us in the account of the Last Supper. When Jesus told Judas to quickly do that which he was planning to do (John 13:27), the disciples automatically supposed that Judas had been instructed by the Lord to give money to the poor.

For some thought, because Judas had the money box, that Jesus had said to him, "Buy those things we need for the feast," or that he should give something to the poor.

John 13:29

From this verse, we see that Jesus was not poor. Instead, He regularly gave *to the poor.*

The
Prosperity
That God
Desires For
His People
Dwells Within
The Pages
Of His Word.

Chapter 7

# ABUNDANCE PROMI$ED

Deuteronomy 28 is made up of two sections that are concisely divided between verses fourteen and fifteen. The first fourteen verses outline the prosperous lifestyle of those who obey God and live in the way that is pleasing to Him. God promises that their livestock and crops will flourish. They will have plenty of provision, as well as an abundance to set aside in savings for the future. No enemy will be able to prosper in any attempt to harm them. God also promises to open the treasures of Heaven to them. They will have the right to live totally debt-free; in fact, they will have more than enough money to be able to lend to others. The promise is that the obedient ones will have lives that are so bountiful, everyone will refer to them as the head and not the tail.

Now, let's take a closer look at the *requirements* for walking in the promised blessings of these first fourteen verses:

> Now it shall come to pass, if you diligently obey the voice of the LORD your God, to observe carefully all His commandments which I command you today, that the LORD your God will set you high above all nations of the earth. And

> all these blessings shall come upon you and overtake you,
> because you obey the voice of the LORD your God.
>
> Deuteronomy 28:1-2

> So you shall not turn aside from any of the words which
> I command you this day, to the right or the left, to go after
> other gods to serve them.
>
> Deuteronomy 28:14

Time and space do not allow a thorough explanation of the second part of Deuteronomy 28, which starts with verse 15 and continues through verse 68. However, it takes only a brief moment to turn to those Scriptures in your own Bible and see how those who are disobedient to God's commandments will have to live, while here on earth. It speaks of poverty, disease, constant distress, with loss after loss, as well as captivity and despair. God promises this continuing chain of calamity will come upon those who are disobedient to His commands.

> But it shall come to pass, if you do not obey the voice of
> the LORD your God, to observe carefully all His command-
> ments and His statutes which I command you today, that all
> these curses will come upon you and overtake you:
>
> Deuteronomy 28:15

The reason for bringing this lengthy discussion about Deuteronomy 28 and its dual promise (one to the obedient and the other to the disobedient) is to ask a simple question: *How did Jesus live His life while He was here on earth?* Did He live in disobedience or in obedience to His Heavenly Father? The Bible answers this question for us.

> And even though Jesus was God's Son, he had to learn from experience what it was like to obey, when obeying meant suffering. <u>It was after he had proved himself perfect in this experience</u> that Jesus became the Giver of eternal salvation to all those who obey him.
>
> Hebrews 5:8-9, *TLB* [emphasis added]

The writer of Hebrews concludes that Jesus walked in perfect obedience to God's commandments and instructions. Scripture further proves the total obedience of Jesus, for the Word of God states that Jesus was without sin, proving that He lived in perfect harmony and obedience to God. Jesus was completely obedient.

> For we do not have a High Priest who cannot sympathize with our weaknesses, but was in all points tempted as we are, yet without sin.
>
> Hebrews 4:15

> And being found in appearance as a man, He humbled Himself and became obedient to the point of death, even the death of the cross.
>
> Philippians 2:8

If Jesus walked the earth as a poor man (as some suppose), it would be the strongest evidence that He lived in disobedience to the commandments of His Heavenly Father (Deuteronomy 28:15-68).

However, if Jesus walked in full obedience, as each of us must admit that He did, then every promise in Deuteronomy 28:1-14 would have to be operational in His life. Because of this truth, our Lord's lifestyle must have been one of flowing abundance, with blessings in the field, in the basket, and in the store (verses 3 and 5, *KJV*). According to this promise, He must have been a lender and not a borrower, as well as everything else Deuteronomy 28:1-14 promises to those who are obedient to God.

## The Disciples Were Not Poor

Did the first disciples consider poverty to be a noble, spiritual trait? Let's take another look at John 13:29:

> For some thought, because Judas had the money box, that Jesus had said to him, "Buy those things we need for the feast," or that he should give something to the poor.
>
> **John 13:29**

This verse makes it evident that the disciples did not consider themselves to be poor, for in this discourse they referred to a group other than themselves as "the poor."

The biblical account states that the disciples of our Lord were men of substance. This becomes obvious when we see the great concern that arose among them when our Lord gave this warning to those who were rich.

> Then Jesus said to His disciples, "Assuredly, I say to you that it is hard for a rich man to enter the kingdom of heaven. And again I say to you, it is easier for a camel to go through the eye of a needle than for a rich man to enter the kingdom of God."
>
> **Matthew 19:23-24**

The next verse shows us that the disciples did not respond to these words in the way that impoverished men would respond.

**When His disciples heard it, they were greatly astonished, saying, <u>"Who then can be saved?"</u>**
**Matthew 19:25 [emphasis added]**

These men who walked in the inner circle of our Lord showed great personal concern, wondering aloud, "If rich people can't be saved, then who can?" Think about it. This response would never, in a thousand years, have come from the mouths of poor men. Quite the contrary, if our Lord's disciples were poor, they would have no doubt started rejoicing that poor people such as themselves could easily enter the kingdom of God.

The Scriptures tell us that when Jesus saw their great concern, He immediately began to assure them that all things are possible with God and that even men of wealth could be saved.

**But Jesus looked at them and said to them, "With men this is impossible, but with God all things are possible."**
**Matthew 19:26**

Notice carefully how our Lord phrases His response to their alarm. Jesus *looked at them* – not at some other group of people – and said *to them* that, with God, even rich men could enter God's kingdom. It is very important to notice that, in this same moment of concern over their wealth, Jesus makes one of the most powerful promises of abundant increase in the entire Bible or anywhere else. He promises His disciples that everyone who invests their precious things into the gospel will receive, in kind, a hundredfold increase.

> …everyone who has left houses or brothers or sisters or father or mother or wife or children or lands, for My name's sake, shall receive a hundredfold, and inherit eternal life.
>
> Matthew 19:29

To get the full impact of this promise, it is necessary to hear it from Mark's account, where Jesus said those who give into the gospel would not have to wait until they got to Heaven to receive the hundredfold increase. He was straightforward in declaring that God would fund this promise *here and now, on earth, in this present life.*

> …Assuredly, I say to you, there is no one who has left house or brothers or sisters or father or mother or wife or children or lands, for My sake and the gospel's, who shall not receive a hundredfold now in this time—houses and brothers and sisters and mothers and children and lands, with persecutions—and in the age to come, eternal life.
>
> Mark 10:29-30

It is obvious from this small portion of Scripture that Jesus really meant it when He said that if we give, it will be given back to us, "good measure, pressed down, shaken together, and running over" (Luke 6:38).

The Scriptures give even more proof that the disciples were not paupers, for it is written in the biblical account that their businesses continued to prosper even as they followed Jesus. The Bible clearly states that, for a period of time after the resurrection, the disciples returned to Galilee and resumed their businesses, having adequate boats, nets, and fishing apparatus awaiting them (John 21). They remained occupied with their businesses until Jesus commanded them to go to Jerusalem and await the advent of the Holy Spirit. It is also recorded in God's Word that the disciples employed hired servants.

> When He had gone a little farther from there, He saw James the son of Zebedee, and John his brother, who also were in the boat mending their nets. And immediately He called them, and they left their father Zebedee in the boat with the hired servants...
>
> **Mark 1:19-20**

# The Apostle Paul Was A Man Of Substance

As we study the financial status of the early disciples, we find that the Apostle Paul had money. The Bible tells us that he was able to generate enough cash flow to allow him to forgo taking offerings whenever it was in the best interest of the gospel outreach to do so (1 Corinthians 9:12). The record also tells us that Paul had his own business of tent making (Acts 18:3), a business that brought an ongoing flow of revenue into his ministry.

It is also interesting to note that when Paul was in prison, under Felix's control, this prominent Roman proctor was after

Paul's money. The Bible tells us that Felix hoped to get a substantial sum of money from Paul in the form of a bribe.

> **Meanwhile he also hoped that money would be given him by Paul, that he might release him. Therefore he sent for him more often and conversed with him.**
>
> Acts 24:26

Common sense tells us that a rich and famous Roman official like the great Felix would not be interested in the apostle's money if it were only a few meager pennies. When considering Felix's interest in bribe money from the Apostle Paul, remember that, as a Roman official, he had access to the financial records of Paul and his family.

Add to this knowledge the fact that the Apostle Paul promised, in writing, to pay all the back wages that a runaway slave named Onesimus owed his master. We read about this in the Book of Philemon. To fully understand the potential size of the debt the apostle pledged to pay, you must realize that, according to Roman law, a runaway slave was required to pay his master a day's wage for each day that he was a runaway.

Some secular writers estimate that Onesimus had been a runaway for as many as ten years. This meant he owed approximately ten years of wages to his master. The letter Onesimus carried back to his master contained Paul's personal, handwritten pledge to pay all that Onesimus might owe.

> But if he [Onesimus] has wronged you or owes anything, put that on my account. I, Paul, am writing with my own hand. I will repay—not to mention to you that you owe me even your own self besides.
>
> **Philemon 18-19**

To say the Apostle Paul was poor, you would have to completely ignore all the information in God's Word to the contrary and look instead to the superstition of religious tradition.

Now, let's address the question that arises from those who would refer to yet another verse out of context.

> I know how to be abased, and I know how to abound. Everywhere and in all things I have learned both to be full and to be hungry, both to abound and to suffer need.
>
> **Philippians 4:12**

There is an easy explanation for the declaration of need that the Apostle Paul makes in this verse. Paul traveled extensively, residing in strange lands and foreign countries for many years at a time. In the day that Paul lived, this kind of extensive traveling would cause him to be physically separated from his material wealth for long periods of time. Add to this the hardship of imprisonment, shipwreck, and the distress of life on the road, and it becomes easy to understand that needs would arise. With this in mind, we see that Paul's declaration of need in no way proves he was a poor man. It was simply a fact of life that came with extensive travel in the first century, when there weren't banks or ATMs available on every corner.

# He That Was Rich Became Poor

Another reason that many believers question whether Jesus had material wealth is a statement the Apostle Paul made about our Lord. In that statement, Paul said that though our Lord was rich, for our sakes He became poor.

> **For you know the grace of our Lord Jesus Christ, that though He was rich, yet for your sakes He became poor, that you through His poverty might become rich.**
>
> **2 Corinthians 8:9**

We can quickly solve the seeming difficulty that arises from this verse by considering two very important things. First, Paul's statement about Jesus becoming poor can easily be explained by pointing out the difference between the life Jesus lived in Heaven and the life He lived while here on earth. Jesus laid aside all of His heavenly powers and riches to become a man.

> **Let this mind be in you which was also in Christ Jesus, who, being in the form of God, did not consider it robbery to be equal with God, but made Himself of no reputation, taking the form of a bondservant, and coming in the likeness of men. And being found in appearance as a man, He humbled Himself and became obedient to the point of death, even the death of the cross.**
>
> **Philippians 2:5-9**

He gave up limitless power, as Creator of the universe, to become a helpless human baby, dependent on others for His complete care. For the first time in eternity, Jesus had to experience the limitations of living within a fleshly, human body on this earth.

Jesus most surely became poor by Heaven's standards, when He was born in Bethlehem. In comparison to Heaven's riches, He entered a universe of poverty. Leaving that splendid place of opulent wealth to come to the spiritual war zone known as earth could easily explain Paul's statement of Jesus' being rich and becoming poor. However, this in no way proves that He became poor by earth's standards. As we have already seen, He was not born into a poor family. Add to this fact that a number of fabulously rich kings lavishly funded His ministry soon after He was born.

> **...when they had come into the house, they saw the young Child with Mary His mother, and fell down and worshiped Him. And when they had opened their treasures, they presented gifts to Him: gold, frankincense, and myrrh.**
>
> **Matthew 2:11**

Also notice that the biblical record reveals there were many financial donors who gave generously and regularly into the ongoing operation of our Lord's earthly ministry.

> **...and certain women who had been healed of evil spirits and infirmities—Mary called Magdalene, out of whom had come seven demons, and Joanna the wife of Chuza, Herod's steward, and Susanna, and many others who provided for Him from their substance.**
>
> **Luke 8:2-3**

There is another even more compelling Bible proof that clarifies the apostle's statement. This becomes evident when we consider that Jesus not only became poor for us, He also became sin for us.

> **For He made Him who knew no sin to be sin for us, that we might become the righteousness of God in Him.**
>
> 2 Corinthians 5:21

Not only that, but the Scriptures also tell us He became sick for us.

> **Surely He has borne our griefs (sicknesses, weaknesses, and distresses) and carried our sorrows and pains [of punishment], yet we [ignorantly] considered Him stricken, smitten, and afflicted by God [as if with leprosy]. But He was wounded for our transgressions, He was bruised for our guilt and iniquities; the chastisement [needful to obtain] peace and well-being for us was upon Him, and with the stripes [that wounded] Him we are healed and made whole.**
>
> Isaiah 53:4-5, *AMP*

These verses tell us of the substitutional death that Jesus suffered on behalf of all mankind. In other words, in His atonement, Jesus actually took our place. He became:

- Sin for us, so that we might be righteous (2 Corinthians 5:21)

- Sickness for us, so that we might be healthy (Isaiah 53:4, 5)

- Poor for us, so that we might be rich (2 Corinthians 8:9)

Now, think about this question for just a moment: Did Jesus walk the earth as a sinner for us? No! He became sin for us at His crucifixion. Did Jesus walk the earth as a sick and diseased man? No! He became sickness for us when He was beaten with many stripes at the time of His crucifixion (1 Peter 2:24). In the same way, our Lord did not walk the earth in poverty. He became poor for us, in His atonement, at the time of the crucifixion.

The ultimate form of poverty Jesus willingly took upon Himself was the complete lack of God's presence, when He took upon Himself our sinful state.

> ..."My God, My God, why have you forsaken me?"
>
> **Matthew 27:46**

No, Jesus did not walk the earth as a poor man. However, at His crucifixion, as a part of His atonement, He was crowned the King of poverty, stripped of all material things, power, authority, health, and even stripped of the presence of God. Jesus became poor on the cross, so that we, through His poverty, might become rich.

With this avalanche of biblical proof, it becomes obvious that Jesus did not come into the world to live as a pauper; neither did He minister as a vagabond. Instead, He had abundant finances to do all that the Father required of Him, as He walked this earth. And His sacrifice on Calvary secured the same inheritance of abundance for every child of God's family!

## You Cannot Receive
## What You Do Not Respect

Jesus clearly revealed why He came to this earth:

> **The thief does not come except to steal, and to kill, and to destroy. <u>I have come that they may have life, and that they may have it more abundantly</u>.**
>
> John 10:10 [emphasis added]

The abundant life is the blood-bought inheritance of every true believer. But an inheritance that is not respected cannot be properly received. We must first know who we are in Christ, and then respect the sacrifice that Jesus made for us, in order to have the freedom to live an abundant life.

### What You Invite, You Respect;
### What You Hold In Contempt Is Presently
### Plotting Its Exodus.

One of the qualities that quickly draws the inheritance of abundance is respect. The man who doesn't understand or respect the supreme sacrifice made for him on the cross cannot possibly be a recipient of the benefits this sacrifice bought. Before you can step into a life of prosperity, you first need to address the respect you have (or do not have) for the sacrifice that purchased your financial freedom. Respect is the cause, and financial freedom is the result. Every kingdom benefit grows proportionately to the level of respect one has for it.

The issue of respect is a key determinism to a man's financial future. Your financial freedom is linked to the degree you respect the price of that freedom. When you remember the extravagant price that Jesus paid to purchase the abundant life for you, you will begin to treat money with respect. The law of respect says that you attract what you respect, and you repel what you disrespect. A faithful steward knows that respecting the increase shows that you respect the One who purchased it for you.

Let's quickly review the rich inheritance and the message of promise that Christ purchased with His life. He promises:

- Abundant life (John 10:10)

- One hundredfold return of houses and land, in this time (Mark 10:30)

- An abundant return on your giving (Luke 6:38)

- Answers to your prayers for your every need and desire (Matthew 7:7-8)

- Forgiveness for sin and the promise of eternal life…provision of all we need for all eternity! (John 3:16)

The Bible is clear about possessing abundance:

- God will provide abundant supply to meet all your needs. *"And my God shall supply all your need according to His riches in glory by Christ Jesus" (Philippians 4:19).*

- Jesus has provided for us bounteously! *"For you know the grace of our Lord Jesus Christ, that though He was rich, yet for your sakes He became poor, that you through His poverty might become rich" (2 Corinthians 8:9).*

- God is ready to provide you with more than you can ever imagine. *"...to know the love of Christ which passes knowledge; that you may be filled with all the fullness of God. Now to Him who is able to do exceedingly abundantly above all that we ask or think, according to the power that works in us..." (Ephesians 3:19, 20).*

- God already gave mankind the best, when He gave us His Son. How could anyone imagine that He would hold back anything else after giving Heaven's Firstborn? *"He who did not spare His own Son, but delivered Him up for us all, how shall He not with Him also freely give us all things?" (Romans 8:32).*

# The Area in Which You Invest Your Time Determines How You Live Your Life.

Chapter 8

# LOOK
# At HEAVEN

Have you noticed that individuals who grow up with loving, responsible parents, who protect and provide for them, have an entirely different way of thinking than those who grow up in poverty (be it financial poverty, emotional poverty, or both)? A constant existence of lack and hardship corrodes a person's heart, perspective, and expectations of life. Conversely, the steady security of knowing one is provided for (and periodically lavished upon) nurtures a person's positive outlooks, beliefs, and expectations for the future, giving him faith and confidence to take the necessary steps to make a difference in this world.

As earthly children, we quickly become familiar with and affected by the lifestyle of our parents. What we see modeled in front of us shapes our thoughts and values, and inevitably, we become an outward reflection of our inner beliefs.

**My Outward Actions
Are Little More Than A Display
Of My Inner Convictions.**

In the same way, a true child of God will *reflect* his Heavenly Father's lifestyle. So, what is God's lifestyle really like?

# Rich God, Rich Environment

From walls of jasper to oceans of purest crystal, God lives in total opulence (Revelation 4:6, 21:18). He surrounds Himself with the most precious of gems and costly stones (Revelation 21:19). God walks on streets of purest gold and chooses giant pearls to serve as the gates that lead to His City (Revelation 21:21). God lavishly uses gold for candlesticks, altars, and the other implements He desires. Exquisite crystal extends from His throne for as far as the eye can see. His extravagant cape fills the entire throne room where He sits, and a myriad of magnificent servant creatures wait upon Him, seeking to fulfill His every desire. He dresses His Son with the finest garment, topped off with a solid gold girdle.

> ...in the midst of the seven lampstands, One like the Son of Man, clothed with a garment down to the feet and girded about the chest with a golden band.
>
> **Revelation 1:13**

To demonstrate the acceptable standard of living that God expected for mankind, please take into account the significance of the first geographic directions He ever gave. Right after Adam and Eve were introduced to the splendid garden in Eden, they were given God's detailed directions to the place where they would find the best gold that existed.

> The name of the first is Pishon; it is the one which skirts
> the whole land of Havilah, where there is gold. And the gold
> of that land is good...
>
> Genesis 2:11-12

Think about the importance of these directions, for God could have given them a map to a number of different locations, some that would have suited the doctrines and traditions of the church much better. It might have been directions to the holy water, or the baptistery, or even the bathrooms. However, God chose, as His first geographic directions to man, to show him how to find the finest gold. This is undeniable proof that God's basic intention for Adam and Eve was to never have to think about provision, but to only think about Him. There is further proof when you realize that He instructed Moses to build the tabernacle of the most costly materials (Exodus 37:15-17).

So, as we have already established, it only stands to reason that God's Son, Jesus Christ, must also be extravagantly provided for, for He is God, and God is the provider and provision of all things. However, declaring that Jesus was rich, as He walked the rocky paths of the Holy Land, really upsets the religious traditionalist. I speak of those who believe the medieval superstition that Jesus came to earth as a poor man, and because of this assumption, also believe that His followers should be poor.

To keep the proper biblical perspective, remember that Jesus was not some poor fellow that God chose to be the leader of the new religion that would be called "Christianity." Jesus is the mighty

Son of God who willingly left the realm of glory to tread the earth in search of His fallen creation.

> **For the Son of Man has come to seek and to save that which was lost.**
>
> **Luke 19:10**

With no biblical basis whatsoever, the deceptive dogma of poverty began to creep into the church shortly after the resurrection of the Lord. The doctrine of poverty enslaves believers, enabling religious institutions to more easily exploit and control their every move, both in the Church and even in their daily lives (since you can't do anything without money). The devil, under the guise of "penitent poverty," has diverted immense amounts of wealth away from the children of God. He has done it through the religious lie that falsely declares to God's church that poverty is the badge that validates the believer's devotion and dedication to God.

In direct contradiction to this lie of the poverty-mongers, Jesus declared that His New Covenant purpose for coming to this earth had nothing to do with bringing poverty, but everything to do with giving mankind *abundant life*.

> **...I have come that they may have life, and that they may have it more abundantly.**
>
> **John 10:10**

# Better Promises

What does it *look* like when God rewards and blesses a believer of the New Covenant? Does that person become elevated upon the nobility of poverty? Or does material plenty follow the blessing of the Lord? To receive just a glimpse of the abundance that would have to come with the better promises of the New Covenant, let's compare just a few of the wealth increases that were received under the old covenant.

> ...Jehoshaphat stood and said, "Hear me, O Judah and you inhabitants of Jerusalem: Believe in the LORD your God, and you shall be established; believe His prophets, and you shall prosper."
>
> 2 Chronicles 20:20

The same portion of Scripture goes on to tell us that, in that very same day, the Israelites did prosper.

> When Jehoshaphat and his people came to take away their spoil, they found among them an abundance of valuables on the dead bodies, and precious jewelry, which they stripped off for themselves, more than they could carry away; and they were three days gathering the spoil because there was so much.
>
> 2 Chronicles 20:25 [emphasis added]

Next, let's examine what the Bible says about the blessing of God in Isaac's life:

> **Then Isaac sowed in that land, and reaped in the same year a hundredfold; and the LORD blessed him. The man began to prosper, and continued prospering until he became very prosperous; for he had possessions of flocks and possessions of herds and a great number of servants. So the Philistines envied him.**
>
> **Genesis 26:12-14**

God's blessing, in Isaac's life, meant that Isaac *increased in every way*, including his material wealth!

In seeing the extravagant way in which these Old Testament saints were blessed, we receive a basis for comparison of just how much greater our financial increase is supposed to be, in the better promises of the New Covenant of the New Testament. No matter how greatly God blessed our forefathers in faith, we of the New Covenant have God's unfailing promise that He will do even greater things for us!

> **But now He has obtained a more excellent ministry, inasmuch as He is also Mediator of a better covenant, which was established on _better promises_.**
>
> **Hebrews 8:6 [emphasis added]**

These promises bring us into a better standing with God and a much better lifestyle through God. This wonderful new life in Christ is supposed to be exactly as the writer of Hebrews declared it. It consists of greater and better promises than the promises for the pre-Christian saints of days gone by, for we have a much better covenant than they.

In spite of the fact that God's Word says New Testament saints will enjoy even better promises than those of the Old Testament, the enemy of our souls (Satan) continues to brainwash religious leaders, causing them to believe and teach that being financially challenged and doing without is somehow a better reward than the Old Testament saints received. They believe this despite the fact that the New Testament gospel totally refutes their teaching. How can deception be so appealing to so many? The Bible tells us that some people wrestle with Scriptures to their own destruction.

> **As also in all his epistles, speaking in them of these things, in which are some things hard to understand, which untaught and unstable people twist to their own destruction, as they do also the rest of the Scriptures.**
>
> **2 Peter 3:16**

Contrary to many religious teachings, the Lord and His disciples certainly did not live as vagabonds begging their way through Galilee and the cities thereabout. There is no biblical proof, whatsoever, that Jesus or any of His disciples ever stood around on the street corner holding up a piece of ancient papyrus with Aramaic words scribbled on it, reading, "Will work for food." On the contrary, the Scriptures tell us that Jesus and His disciples had an abundant supply of everything they needed. They had more than enough to enable them to assemble large gatherings, conduct mass meetings, and properly and expeditiously take care of their businesses, as well as running a highly visible ministry. Not only that, but instead of begging for food, the biblical record states that they regularly fed tens of thousands of hungry people. Friend, our rich Father wants us to operate in this same realm of abundance!

## Increased By Seedtime And Harvest

The Law of Seedtime and Harvest is further proof that, from the very beginning, God had increase in mind for His children. God established this covenantal law in Genesis:

> **While the earth remains, Seedtime and harvest, Cold and heat, Winter and summer, And day and night Shall not cease.**
>
> **Genesis 8:22**

Seedtime and harvest exists primarily as an avenue for God to get fruit (money) to abound to the account of His dear children.

> **Now you Philippians know also that in the beginning of the gospel, when I departed from Macedonia, no church shared with me concerning giving and receiving but you only. For even in Thessalonica, you sent aid once and again for my necessities. Not that I seek the gift, <u>but I seek the fruit that abounds to your account.</u>**
>
> **Philippians 4:15-17 [emphasis added]**

God rewards us for believing and honoring Him and then activating His principle of seedtime and harvest in our lives.

> **Honor the LORD with your possessions, and with the firstfruits of all your increase; so your barns will be filled with plenty, and your vats will overflow with new wine.**
>
> **Proverbs 3:9-10**

When we believe and activate this key principle in our lives, God gets involved in our finances. He reveals His wisdom concerning prosperity and gives our hands the power to get wealth. He gives us ways to prosper (such as creative ideas and witty inventions), He teaches us how to make a profit, and perhaps most importantly, He teaches us why He wants us to prosper – so that He may establish His covenant.

> **I wisdom dwell with prudence, and find out knowledge of witty inventions.**
>
> **Proverbs 8:12, *KJV***

> **Thus says the LORD, your Redeemer, The Holy one of Israel: "I am the LORD your God, Who teaches you to profit, Who leads you by the way you should go."**
>
> **Isaiah 48:17**

> **And you shall remember the LORD your God, for it is He who gives you power to get wealth, that He may establish His covenant which He swore to your fathers, as it is this day.**
>
> **Deuteronomy 8:18**

# Partaking Of
# Heaven's Lifestyle

Becoming the child of a rich God is a journey, an ongoing process. Nevertheless, I must tell you that it is a journey fraught with pitfalls and challenges, because people have a very perverted and wrong idea about prosperity. They think that it is all about ministers being after their money.

Friend, a minister who is faithful and obedient to his call will not damn you to a lifetime of lack by telling you that God wants you to have nothing to do with prosperity. Instead, he will teach you how to step into your inheritance in Christ, as well as how to not fall away, once God's Word delivers prosperity to you.

In Ecclesiastes 6:1-2, we see the picture of a man who does not partake of God's wisdom concerning prosperity:

> There is an evil which I have seen under the sun, and it is common among men. A man to whom God has given riches and wealth and honor, so that he lacks nothing for himself of all he desires; yet God does not give him power to eat of it, but a foreigner consumes it. This is vanity, and it is an evil affliction.
>
> **Ecclesiastes 6:1-2**

Note that God gave everything when He gave Jesus and His Word. God is not withholding the power to eat of wealth; it is up to us to pursue, unlock, and perform the revelation that is already given to us through His Word and His Spirit.

By contrast, Ecclesiastes 5:18-20 depicts the person who has availed himself of the knowledge and power of God's wisdom concerning finances and prosperity:

> Here is what I have seen: it is good and fitting for one to eat and drink, and to enjoy the good of all his labor in which he toils under the sun all the days of his life which God gives him; for it is his heritage. As for every man to whom God has given riches and wealth, and given him power to eat of it, to receive his heritage and rejoice in his labor – this is the gift of God. For he will not dwell unduly on the days of his life, because God keeps him busy with the joy of his heart.
>
> Ecclesiastes 5:18-20

## Roadblocks To Receiving

Since God has richly provided, through His Son, the means by which every believer can walk in abundance, why do we see so many Christians struggling in the grips of poverty and lack? Let's look at just a partial list of roadblocks to receiving God's best for our lives:

- Misinformation
- Ignorance
- Laziness
- Misperception
- False doctrine

Let's face it – the devil wants to steal your inheritance. The driving force that brought Satan into disharmony and total rebellion was his envy of man and man's God-given nature (the nature that makes man like God). He will do everything in his power to prevent you from stepping into the inheritance that is rightfully yours as a child of God. The Bible proves that *the devil is the father of the poverty doctrine,* for it records that Satan was the first one to ever proclaim the dismal doctrine of poverty and insufficiency.

> **And the LORD God commanded the man, saying, "Of every tree of the garden you may freely eat..."**
>
> **Genesis 2:16**

> **Now the serpent was more cunning than any beast of the field which the LORD God had made. And he said to the woman, "Has God indeed said, 'You shall not eat of every tree of the garden'?"**
>
> **Genesis 3:1**

It's time we stop listening to the whispered lies of the devil. Your previous environment and circumstances can no longer keep you from prospering. You are a citizen in good standing of God's opulent kingdom of light (Philippians 3:20). With the wealth that God has in reserve for you, you will be able to accomplish all of the wonderful projects He has planned for you. But, you must allow the truth of God's Word to open your eyes, because it is impossible to perform beyond the boundaries of your inner image.

## It Is Impossible To Avoid The Behavior Created By Your Self-Image.

Look closely at the following scriptural examples:

- *Mark 7:25-30* – The woman believed Jesus could help her daughter. Her inward picture dictated her behavior.

- *Mark 5:25-34* – The woman believed Christ could heal her infirmity. Her inward picture dictated her behavior.

- *1 Kings 17:8-16* – When the widow believed the circumstances, she hoarded, which brought lack; when she believed God, she willingly gave, which opened the door to prosperity.

When you sincerely believe God's Word and are doing your best to follow Him, you will be drawn into a process of transformation that will steadily change you into God's likeness.

> **But we all, with unveiled face, beholding as in a mirror the glory of the Lord, are being transformed into the same image from glory to glory, just as by the Spirit of the Lord.**
>
> **2 Corinthians 3:18**

## Meditation

We will examine this process of transformation, in greater depth, in the next chapter. For now, carefully consider this: *The most important function, on any given day, is the intake of Bible doctrine; everything in life depends on it and nothing in life is worthwhile without it.*

## Meditation On God's Word
## Is The Avenue Through Which
## Information Becomes Revelation.

The word "meditate" simply means "to ponder." Meditation, by definition, must be systematic, consistent, and repetitive – a constant "turning it over" in your mind until it paints a picture.

## It Is Only When The Information On
## The Pages Of God's Word Becomes Real
## That It Will Change Your Life.

When we make God's Law our meditation, we will gain revelation, which will guide us in making wise decisions, direct us in the way or path to follow, and cause us to prosper.

> Oh, how I love Your law! It is my meditation all the day.
>
> Psalm 119:97

> Blessed is the man Who walks not in the counsel of the ungodly, Nor stands in the path of sinners, Nor sits in the seat of the scornful; But his delight is in the law of the LORD, And in His law he meditates day and night. He shall be like a tree Planted by the rivers of water, That brings forth its fruit in its season, Whose leaf also shall not wither; And whatever he does shall prosper.
>
> Psalm 1:1-3

This Book of the Law shall not depart from your mouth, but you shall meditate in it day and night, that you may observe to do according to all that is written in it. For then you will make your way prosperous, and then you will have good success.

Joshua 1:8

Don't copy the behavior and customs of this world, but let God transform you into a new person by changing the way you think. Then you will know what God wants you to do, and you will know how good and pleasing and perfect his will really is.

Romans 12:2, *NLT*

## God's Greatest Pleasure

When we allow God's Word to change the way we think about money, something wonderful begins to take place *inside* us. Instead of focusing on what we don't have, we find gratitude rising within us for what we do have. Instead of feeling the grip of fear, we find faith. Instead of resigning ourselves to the chains of our past, we experience hope and expectation for the future!

But without faith it is impossible to please Him, for he who comes to God must believe that He is, and that He is a rewarder of those who diligently seek Him.

Hebrews 11:6

You will discover that expectation plays a key role in your ability to step into the abundance God has for you. For instance, did you expect forgiveness to come when you confessed your sin to God? Of course you did! In the same way, you can expect a harvest to manifest when you give your seed.

## Expectation Is The Environment
## That Allows Seed to Grow.

When we strip ourselves of expectation, we rob God of one of the only pleasures He knows. Why is this true? Because God's greatest pleasure is to be believed!

> Let them shout for joy and be glad, Who favor my righteous cause; And let them say continually, "Let the LORD be magnified, Who has pleasure in the prosperity of His servant."

**Psalm 35:27**

The evidence is overwhelming: God gives both *spiritual and financial* wealth to His children. Poverty is simply not a biblical principle. It is time for God's children to stop believing that poverty is what God wants for their lives!

Friend, *poverty is not God's perfect will for any human.* To live daily on the brink of insufficiency, and claim that it is God's plan, is a spiritual mistake. As we study God's Word, one truth keeps emerging: God has a people, and God takes care of His people *in the spiritual, the physical, and the financial realms.* Our Father is the ultimate provider!

# Prosperity Is An Internal Recognition Before It Is Ever An External Possession.

Chapter 9

# THE BATTLE WITHIN THE MIND

Friend, if you are a believer, then you are the child of the King of kings. You were born into God's kingdom to be the son or daughter of royalty and to enjoy all the benefits thereof. The children of God are the people of the *greater works* (John 14:12). Not only that, but we are also the recipients of a better covenant and better promises (Hebrews 8:6).

> **But now He has obtained a more excellent ministry, inasmuch as He is also Mediator of a better covenant, which was established on better promises.**
>
> **Hebrews 8:6**

Jesus wants you to experience more than just getting inside the front door of Heaven. He said, "I will give you the keys *of* the kingdom" (Matthew 16:19). In other words, He said, "I want you to experience, in this life, every treasure and promise that is hidden inside My Word, including the blessing of financial abundance!"

Access to the precious treasures of God's Word is not given in a casual or haphazard manner. I must apply all that I am to the search! I must continually ask, seek, and knock (Matthew 7:7). I must learn to love God and to esteem His Word *more than anything else in life.*

Ironically, this may be one of your greatest challenges, if you've gone to church your whole life. If you've grown up in the church, you may have begun to see the Word of God from a carnal perspective: "Well, this is just church. This is just what we do at church." You may not understand that *your whole life* needs to conform to God's Word.

## The Bible Is Not Just Another Book; It Is The Owner's Manual For Life.

At this point, you may be thinking, "Okay, I know I've been listening to the voice of my unrenewed mind, as it torments me with thoughts of hopelessness, defeat, disappointment, despair, poverty, and fear of lack. But, now that I've seen the overwhelming biblical evidence that God wants me to prosper, how do I make it work for me? How do I discard all the erroneous traditions and doctrines about the desirability of a lifetime of poverty? What steps can I take to allow the Word of God to renew my mind and transform my finances and my life?"

Friend, I have some very practical yet life-changing answers for you. Please continue with me, as I share with you the keys to stepping into your life as a child of our rich Father.

# What Do You Believe?

As I discussed earlier, the most important key has to do with what we believe. In the thirteenth chapter of the Book of Numbers, we see that all but two of the nearly three million Israelites believed that they were "grasshoppers" in the eyes of the giants in the land, and therefore, never entered the Promised Land. However, Joshua and Caleb believed God's promise, and eventually, became prosperous and successful.

Let's look at Abraham. God said He would bless Abraham and cause him to become a blessing to others (Genesis 12:2). He also said that Abraham's descendants would be as numerous as the stars of the sky (Genesis 15:5). The Bible says, "Abraham believed God, and it was accounted to him for righteousness" (Romans 4:3).

## Your Future Prosperity
## Lies In The Present Confines Of Your Mind.

This is true for any area of your life, including your finances. Whatever you predominantly give your thoughts to will create your future. As God's children, it is His desire that we give our thoughts predominantly to Him and to His Word, so that our futures can be abundantly prospered (Isaiah 55:8-9).

This dynamic principle was revealed to Joshua at a time when he was feeling quite fearful and overwhelmed. His mentor, Moses, had just died. God gave Joshua the enormous assignment of taking Moses' place and stepping into the position of leading the Israelites into the Promised Land. The responsibility was daunting, and he really needed some major reassurance.

So, God told Joshua, "Now, look, I know you're afraid. I know you want to quit. I know you're not sure if you can lead these people. But, Joshua, you can do this – and now, I'm going to tell you how."

"This is what you do," He said. "You put My Word in front of your eyes, in your thoughts, and in your mouth – meditate on it day and night. Stay inside there long enough for My Word to paint you a picture. Once you can see yourself in that picture, you will succeed and prosper" (author's paraphrase of Joshua 1:8).

Let's read this passage, found in Joshua 1:7-9:

> **Only be strong and very courageous, that you may observe to do according to all the law which Moses My servant commanded you; do not turn from it to the right hand or to the left, that you may prosper wherever you go. This Book of the Law shall not depart from your mouth, but you shall meditate in it day and night, that you may observe to do according to all that is written in it. For then you will make your way prosperous, and then you will have good success. Have I not commanded you? Be strong and of good courage; do not be afraid, nor be dismayed, for the LORD your God is with you wherever you go.**
>
> **Joshua 1:7-9**

It's important to note that prosperity does not solely consist of one's possessions. God did not design prosperity merely for us to attain nice cars, expensive jewelry, or fancy homes. He designed it, so that, like Joshua, we would have *more than enough to fulfill the assignment that He has given to us.*

You see, God calls us into His prosperity and abundance, so that He can use us as paymasters for His kingdom purposes – but without a clear mental picture, we cannot complete this assignment.

> **...do not be conformed to this world, but be transformed by the renewing of your mind, <u>that you may prove what is that good and acceptable and perfect will of God</u>.**
>
> **Romans 12:2 [emphasis added]**

Remember, financial freedom will not come overnight. The promises of God didn't come that way for Abraham, Isaac, Jacob, or Joshua. Making the necessary mental changes is a process. Renewing your mind *begins* the process, but you must begin it right now.

Whatever God does, He does it step by step. Friend, don't believe people when they tell you that He does it overnight, or that all you need to do is sow your seed and you will see an instantaneous miracle. Don't let any get-rich-quick scheme convince you that there is a miracle answer, because it's not true – it doesn't work that way! (Proverbs 13:11, 28:20, *NLT*). I wish there was a silver bullet to all of this, but there isn't. You must do things God's way, and then God will begin His work in the realm of your thought life.

## Your Thoughts Are The Compass That Guides The Ship Of Life Into Your Port Of Desire.

Where do you want to go in life? What do you want to achieve? Some of you just wish that you had all of your bills paid in full. Others wish you had more than enough money, so that you could help others. I'm sure you've thought, "If I could just win the lottery, I'd pay off my house, my car, and other people's debt as well!" We've all fantasized about those kinds of things. But we must ask ourselves, "Where is the thought compass that is guiding my ship?"

I know that when I was younger – captive to drugs, alcohol, and all that goes along with them – I didn't think much about where I wanted to go. I assumed that I would end up a failure, like the generations before me, and I made daily decisions based on those assumptions. But remember, friend, **the thoughts on which we dwell form the compass that guides our ship towards success or failure, prosperity or poverty.**

## What Do You Focus On?

People do not attract what they want; they attract what they *think*. Whatever you focus on grows. It becomes bigger in your mind and more influential in your actions and decision-making processes. Because I know this to be true, I have made it a daily discipline to ask myself this question: *"Have I been focusing on the problems, or have I been focusing on God?"*

It is foolish to expect abundance and success in our lives if the majority of our thoughts focus on lack and failure. We will never experience prosperity if our thoughts are endlessly rehearsing our regrets, bitterness, or hopelessness over being impoverished. *Every thought that you agree with becomes a powerful magnet; drawing into your life the manifested reality of the picture it holds.*

## Our Lives Will Always Move In The Direction Of Our Most Dominant Thoughts.

Now, this is an extremely valuable principle to know, if you want to create the future you desire, rather than just passively say, "Whatever will be will be." Are you tired of your present life situations? Do you want your life to move in a different direction? Then what you must do is focus on the abundant inheritance purchased for you by the blood of our Lord, rather than on the circumstances of lack that surround you. *Whatever you focus on grows.* The more you place your thoughts on your inheritance in Christ, the more your desire to attain it grows.

Usually, people's thoughts are focused on their desire to *leave* something, rather than to *move toward* something. For example, most people want to leave financial headaches and pressures behind and live in the security of abundance, but they focus on the stress and pressure of the bills that aren't paid, the clothes they can't buy, etc., rather than focusing on becoming good stewards of what God has given them by eliminating poverty-producing practices and making wise financial decisions. Their thoughts are focused on lack, and yet, they expect their lives to move in the direction of abundance. It is impossible! **Your life will always go in the direction of your most dominant thoughts.** Therefore, you must focus on where you want to go, **not** on what you'd like to leave behind.

> ...we do not look at the things which are seen, but at the
> things which are not seen. For the things which are seen are
> temporary, but the things which are not seen are eternal.
>
> 2 Corinthians 4:18

You are doing one of two things at all times. You are either looking at the things that you can see, or you are looking at the things that you may not see yet, but know, from God's Word, to be true. You have to ask yourself in every situation, "Which one am I looking at? Am I looking at what I see, or am I looking at what I don't see?" For the things which are seen are temporary.

## Your Future Success
## Is Created By Your Present Focus.

Your knee-jerk reaction to my words may be to insist, "But, don't you see all the horrible things that are going on? The economy is a mess, people are losing their houses, their jobs, and their health benefits, and in looking at the political and financial horizon, it only appears to be getting worse!"

I didn't say I don't see them. I said I'm not *looking* at them. It's when you *look* at them that you get depressed. So, I'm not going to look at them.

"Aren't you just in denial?"

I'm not denying that those situations exist, but they are the *outside picture*. They are *a* truth. They are *temporary, subject to change, and not to be trusted.* As I spend more time focusing on the unseen, eternal picture, the visible distractions will become *invisible* and *unimportant.*

What I choose to look at and focus on is the picture of success and victory that the Word of God has painted inside of me. That picture is eternal, and it *will not change*. It is *"The Truth," and it is the only thought to be trusted.* When this is my focus, true change happens.

## Freedom Is An Internal Journey, Not The Absence Of External Torment.

Any abundance or increase in life occurs only through soul prosperity. When we fill our minds with His Word, our souls begin to prosper. **Prosperity does not happen in the external realm, before first happening in our minds.** This is where most well-meaning believers fail. We must begin, today, to infiltrate our minds with Heaven's thoughts. Only when we are focused on God's kingdom-thoughts will we truly be on the path to living our lives as children of our rich Heavenly Father.

You see, God has nothing against our having material things, as long as they're not our focus in life. We must seek first the kingdom of God before we can ever enjoy the pleasures of this life. Jesus taught His disciples, saying,

> **Seek first the kingdom of God and His righteousness, and all these things shall be added to you.**
>
> **Matthew 6:33**

In the *New Living Translation*, it tells us this:

> **He will give you all you need, from day to day, if you live for Him and make the Kingdom of God your primary concern.**
>
> **Matthew 6:33, *NLT***

Unfortunately, most Christians either see themselves as poor servants to a poor god, or they start seeking God's hand of provision, rather than seeking His face and His kingdom. I want to encourage you to focus on God's kingdom, not on your prosperity. Focus on the kingdom of God, with a strong subtitle of God's prosperity. You see, if you seek first God's kingdom and His righteousness, all the rest will be added to you. It's coming, friend! All things will be added to you. Never give up! Never give in. All things *will* be added to you.

## What Are You Saying?

If you don't keep your mind renewed, and your mouth full of God's Word, your old, impoverished, dead man will haunt and dominate you.

### We Must Never Give Life
### To What God Has Put To Death.

You need to keep the dead in its spiritual grave. How? Continual input of "living thoughts" (God's Word) will push out the dead thoughts. Continual speaking of "The Answer" will push out the problems.

> The mouth of the righteous man utters wisdom, and his tongue speaks what is just. The law of his God is in his heart; his feet do not slip.
>
> **Psalm 37:30-31, *NIV***

Do not snatch the word of truth from my mouth, for I have put my hope in your laws. I will always obey your law, for ever and ever. I will walk about in freedom, for I have sought out your precepts. I will speak of your statutes before kings and will not be put to shame.

Psalm 119:43-46, *NIV*

Set a guard, O LORD, over my mouth; Keep watch over the door of my lips. Do not incline my heart to any evil thing, To practice wicked works With men who work iniquity; And do not let me eat of their delicacies.

Psalm 141:3-4

Proverbs 6:2 says, *"You are snared by the words of your mouth; you are taken by the words of your mouth."* Pay attention to your thoughts and your words throughout the day. When you notice a negative thought of poverty and lack, replace it with God's thought. When you install God's thoughts into your mental hardware, they will erase all previously diseased or contaminated thoughts.

## Your Spirit Will Produce
## That Which It Hears
## Your Mouth Speak.

As we saw earlier, Joshua was feeling very inadequate about stepping into the shoes of Moses. God asked Joshua, "Do you want to know how to succeed where Moses failed?" God's instructions to Joshua were very clear:

> This Book of the Law <u>shall not depart from your mouth</u>,
> but you shall meditate in it day and night, that you may ob-
> serve to do according to all that is written in it. For then you
> will make your way prosperous, and then you will have good
> success.
>
> Joshua 1:8 [emphasis added]

And now, God is asking us, "Do you want to know the secret to a prosperous, successful future? *This Book must never depart out of your mouth.* You must meditate on it day and night, so that you'll see yourself doing according to all that's written therein; for then *you*...will make your way prosperous and then *you*...will have good success."

## Heart-Pictures

God tells us that if we will *constantly* meditate, day and night, on the Word of God, it will begin to build a "heart-picture" for us, and when it does, *we* will make our way prosperous and have good success. God wants us to stay inside of His Word long enough for it to create snapshots of success within our hearts and minds. These images are the starting points of your financial deliverance. When you begin to *see* what God has for you, you will begin to *act* in such a way that you'll break free from the mental pressures and the mistakes of your past.

Joshua understood how crucial it was to get a picture. The Bible tells us:

> So the LORD spoke to Moses face to face, as a man speaks to his friend. And he would return to the camp, but his servant Joshua the son of Nun, a young man, did not depart from the tabernacle.
>
> Exodus 33:11

Why did Joshua stay in the tent of meeting long after Moses had left? Because he needed a picture. The presence of God is what brings the picture. **It is only when the information on the pages of God's Word becomes *real* that it will change your life.** As you continually look into and meditate on the Word of God for your answers to every situation of life, the Word will paint a picture for you. That heart-picture will change the way you think. It will change the way you live. It will change everything about you. And there is no other way for that inner transformation to take place.

This process of renewing one's mind (Romans 12:2) is so much more than simple memorization of Scriptures. A person can memorize and quote thousands of Scriptures, but that doesn't mean he knows any of them. We must go beyond "knowing it" mentally, and let it paint a picture in our hearts.

Many people who profess to be Christians "know" a lot of Scriptures, but continue to live in poverty and sin. **If we "know" a lot of Scriptures, but we're not staying in them long enough for them to paint a picture, then we begin to think that God's Word doesn't work.** Our perception becomes perverted, because our inside character is not keeping up with our outside intake of knowledge. If we really want to get the picture from a Scripture, we should choose to meditate on one Scripture hundreds of times, instead of reading hundreds of Scriptures one time!

If a person is living without pictures, it's because he is passing through what I like to call "The Death Valley of Religion." Remember this: Religion is the death valley of your spiritual life. It's where you know things in your head, but cannot produce them in your life. Religion downloads the Word into your mind, but doesn't install it into your heart. Unless it is installed into the hard drive of your heart, through meditation and confession of God's Word, it cannot produce.

David reiterates the importance of meditation, in the following Psalms:

> **Oh, how I love Your law! It is my meditation all the day.**
> **Psalm 119:97**

> **But his delight is in the law of the LORD, And in His law he meditates day and night. He shall be like a tree Planted by the rivers of water, That brings forth its fruit in its season, Whose leaf also shall not wither; And whatever he does shall prosper.**
> **Psalm 1:2-3**

Your heart-picture is the key. Whose brush are you allowing to paint your heart-picture?

## Guard Your Heart

Every time the devil attacks your mind with an oppressive thought of poverty and lack, you stand at a fork in the road. Each time, you must make the choice either to believe and speak *the thought* or to believe and speak *the Word.* And each time, God's Word stands as a clear, immovable signpost, pointing the way to the path you should take; your task is simply to obey.

> **I call heaven and earth as witnesses today against you, that I have set before you life and death, blessing and cursing; therefore choose life, that both you and your descendants may live; that you may love the LORD your God, that you may obey His voice, and that you may cling to Him, for He is your life and the length of your days; and that you may dwell in the land which the LORD swore to your fathers, to Abraham, Isaac, and Jacob, to give them.**
>
> **Deuteronomy 30:19-20**

Remember, *the choice is yours to make.* Whichever thought you choose to believe, whether positive (believing God's Word) or negative (believing you are doomed to be poor), it *will* produce a harvest in your life, whether you want it to or not!

### Your Heart Is The Soil
### Where Your Thoughts Become
### The Seeds That Create Your Future.

Please think about that for a moment. Your thoughts actually become the seeds that create your future. Based on what you have been thinking lately, what kind of future can you expect? When you imagine your life one, ten, or twenty-five years from now, do you see yourself financially struggling to get by, or do you picture you and your family living a prosperous, successful life?

> **Keep your heart with all diligence, for out of it spring the issues of life.**
>
> Proverbs 4:23

Above everything else, keep (guard, protect, defend, and put a fence around) your heart! Never allow your heart to be bludgeoned, pierced, assailed, or attacked by any words that will keep you from believing that God wants to bless your life and the generations that come after you. Why is this so important? Because the voices and thoughts that enter your mind are *seeds*. And seeds are designed to produce a harvest.

## It Is Impossible To Escape The Harvest Of Our Most Present Thoughts.

What thoughts are most present in your mind throughout the day? Are they thoughts that God wants you to be blessed? Or are they thoughts that, since your father and grandfather were poor, you are going to follow in their footsteps and be poor just as well?

Believe me, I know what that's like! I didn't grow up with a silver spoon in my mouth. I grew up with a poverty mindset, which was predetermined to bring me to failure. I didn't even know how poor we were until people told me that we didn't have anything.

I'll never forget how the landlord came banging on the door when my parents weren't home, attempting to gain entrance to where my brothers and I were. He would pound and pound and pound for hours, and we would sit there, just shivering and shaking in fear, because we didn't know what he was going to do (my parents had told us that he was crazy). I didn't grow up in a home where a mom put on an apron, cooked dinner, washed the clothes, and looked nice for Dad. I grew up in a place that was riddled with alcoholism…but I didn't want it to be that way with my life.

However, I knew that before my life could ever go forward, it would have to break down first. And that is what happened. My life broke down, and my mind caved in. I went through a nervous breakdown and ended up in a mental institution. The doctors told me I had a deep character disorder and there was nothing they could do for me. And then, Jesus entered my life, and everything changed. I began to passionately focus on and pursue God and His Word.

## Thought-Seeds

You are a warehouse of seeds, and you create your future by the seeds that you sow. You have a choice over which "thought-seeds" you plant, where they are planted, or whether they are ever planted at all. You have a choice to reject thought-seeds that are destined to produce unwanted harvests. When you plant those thought-seeds, your heart becomes the fertile soil where they grow up and produce fruit in your life.

You see, I landed in a mental institution because of the thought-seeds that I had sown in my mind. Some of them, I consciously sowed. Others, I subconsciously allowed to invade my heart and my life, letting them go unchallenged. Looking back on that time in my life, I have realized an important truth:

## Any Thought That Is Left Unchallenged Is Established As Fact.

For me, *fear* went unchallenged. I thought it would just go away. But if you don't make it go away, it's not going away. For you, it might be something else. For many people, it has to do with this issue of financial turmoil. If you don't believe that God wants you to prosper, then that thought is established as fact, and you'll find evidence to support your thinking.

"After all," you might be thinking, "look at all the starving people in the world; look at the terrible economy, and look at how many people are out of work…"

Friend, none of these things mean that God wants you to be poor. Remember, if the world wants to go into a recession, you can choose not to participate!

How can we win the nations to Christ if we don't have the money to support evangelistic outreaches around the world? It doesn't happen unless Christians prosper and then tithe and give into evangelism, to see the rest of the world saved. Other world religions are succeeding in converting people simply because they have the finances to do it. Therefore, in the interest of winning the world for Christ, you and I must challenge the thought that "poverty is a virtue." So, how do we challenge a thought? The Bible tells us:

> **For though we walk in the flesh, we do not war according to the flesh. For the weapons of our warfare are not carnal but mighty in God for pulling down strongholds, casting down arguments and every high thing that exalts itself against the knowledge of God, bringing every thought into captivity to the obedience of Christ...**
>
> 2 Corinthians 10:3-5

When you don't reject negative beliefs, they begin to dig their claws deeper and deeper, down on the inside of you. When you don't reject a wrong thought, it begins to develop a hold on you. When you allow negative thinking to remain in your mind, and you let it go unchallenged, it will soon become your master. How do you reject a negative thought? By replacing it with a promise from God's Word.

Let me give you an example. Instead of believing that God wants you to be poor, replace that thought with Deuteronomy 8:18, and repeatedly say to yourself, "It is God who gives me the power to get wealth...It is God who gives me the power to get wealth..." How long will that take? It'll take as long as you are willing to hold off planting that thought of poverty in your heart.

You must become *steadfast and unwavering* in your meditation and confession of God's Word. It's not something that can come and go. To be effective, it has to become an everyday exercise.

Don't do anything by discipline. Do it by habit. Like all habits, this one is formed through repetition. As you become consistent in your meditation on God's Word, you'll discover that its benefits are contagious – they spread to everything in your life! It's what you do *consistently* that will determine the outcome of your life. In order to break free of the spirit of poverty that has bound you, God's Word must continually be in your mouth. If you're going to speak, say what God says; then watch your life for the inconsistencies of your actions and words. Remember this principle:

## The Instruction You Follow Will Determine The Outcome Of Your Life.

Follow the instruction of God's Word, and then *you will make your way prosperous, and no man or devil in hell can stop you!*

Give yourself unreservedly to meditation on the Word of God. Ponder it and orally recite it, both day and night, until it paints a brilliantly clear picture of prosperity and abundance within you. Then, refusing to look at what you see with your natural eyes, focus instead on what you see with your spiritual eyes. As you do, you will be able to laugh at the days ahead, for you will already know the inexpressible blessings that the future holds for you!

# Action Is The 'Bridge' That Links The World Of Desire With The Land Of Fulfillment.

Chapter 10

# OUR RIGHTFUL INHERITANCE

As we have discovered from close examination of God's Word, much of the church today is replete with good intentions but bad doctrine. The false doctrine of poverty continues to propagate, as more and more religious leaders make the same mistake of taking the vow of poverty as well as passing it on to future generations. We, the church, must recognize that neither poverty nor sickness are God's perfect will for His children.

> Beloved, I pray that you may prosper in all things and be in health, just as your soul prospers.
>
> 3 John 2

## Christians Are Not Commissioned To Be Poor

Let us turn our attention to another one of the misunderstood Scripture passages used to support the erroneous teaching that Jesus wants His church to live in poverty. It comes from a

133

complete misunderstanding of why Jesus instructed His disciples not to take any money as they went forth to minister for Him (Luke 10:4). For some reason, the poor children of the poor god mistakenly perceive themselves as having received these same instructions from their god. They believe they have been given a mandate that requires them to walk in poverty while evangelizing the world.

> **Carry neither moneybag, knapsack, nor sandals; and greet no one along the road. But whatever house you enter, first say, "Peace to this house." And if a son of peace is there, your peace will rest on it; if not, it will return to you. And remain in the same house, eating and drinking such things as they give, for the laborer is worthy of his wages. Do not go from house to house. Whatever city you enter, and they receive you, eat such things as are set before you. And heal the sick there, and say to them, "The kingdom of God has come near to you."**
>
> **Luke 10:4-9**

As soon as you put all this in its proper context, it immediately becomes clear that *on this particular journey,* Jesus instructed His disciples not to take any provisions or money with them. He did it because they were going into the "house of a friend" (the lost sheep of the house of Israel). Jewish tradition and etiquette dictated that servants of God would be received as honored guests in the Jewish villages they visited.

As strange as it may seem (in light of religious superstitions to the contrary), Jesus never once commanded His New Testament church to go into the world with this same commission. The Bible tells us that near the end of His earthly walk, Jesus cancelled this first commission and completely recommissioned the church before sending them into the Gentile world to preach the gospel.

> And He said to them, "When I sent you without money bag, knapsack, and sandals, did you lack anything?" So they said, "Nothing." Then He said to them, "But now, he who has a money bag, let him take it, and likewise a knapsack; and he who has no sword, let him sell his garment and buy one."
>
> Luke 22:35-36

Jesus obviously intends for His church to be financially well-equipped for the completion of our assignment. Let's review our definition of *prosperity*:

## Prosperity Is Having Enough Of God's Provision To Fulfill The Assignment He Gave To You.

Here is a simple truth about today's world that we all know from experience: it requires money to do just about anything. We need money to secure property, to build proper buildings, and to furnish and equip them for ministry. We need sufficient money to gather the resources necessary to feed the hungry, clothe the naked, visit the prisoners, and supply the needs of widows and orphans. We also need abundant finances to complete the Great Commission, which commands the church to go into all the world and preach the gospel.

> And Jesus came and spoke to them, saying, "All author-
> ity has been given to Me in heaven and on earth. Go
> therefore and make disciples of all the nations, baptizing
> them in the name of the Father and of the Son and of the
> Holy Spirit, teaching them to observe all things that I have
> commanded you; and lo, I am with you always, even to the
> end of the age." Amen.
>
> Matthew 28:18-20

Everyone knows that airlines rarely allow people to travel at
no cost. Automobiles, busses, and trucks (as well as the fuel it
takes to operate them) cost big money. The fact is that we live in a
world that requires money to operate. Yes, God does promise
miracles, but even with all the miracles, it still takes big money to
evangelize the world. If you go to a foreign country and don't speak
the language, you will have difficulty conducting any meaningful
conversation with the locals. However, if you have the funds, you
can hire an interpreter or pay the tuition to learn at a language
school. If you don't have a good supply of the currency of the world
system, it will be difficult to get much of anything done toward
evangelizing the world. Remember, the Word of God tells us that
*"money answers everything"* (Ecclesiastes 10:19).

## The Early Church Had Wealth

As to the biblical account of finances in the early church,
Scripture tells us that the first church at Jerusalem controlled a
large block of financial wealth. In the Book of Acts, all the believ-

ers in Jerusalem sold everything they had and placed the cash in a common treasury. Estimates of the number of church members run anywhere from approximately 11,000 to as high as 20,000. With this many members selling their possessions and laying them down at the feet of the apostles, there were, no doubt, very large amounts of money in the control of the church at Jerusalem. This single act of giving created enough ready cash to bless every believer in the church, properly supplying every requirement that might have arisen.

> And with great strength and ability and power the apostles delivered their testimony to the resurrection of the Lord Jesus, and great grace (loving-kindness and favor and goodwill) rested richly upon them all. <u>Nor was there a destitute or needy person among them,</u> for as many as were owners of lands or houses proceeded to sell them, and one by one they brought (gave back) the amount received from the sales and laid it at the feet of the apostles (special messengers). Then distribution was made according as anyone had need.
>
> Acts 4:33-35, *AMP* [emphasis added]

This is one of the most interesting statements in the Word of God. It declares that the church at Jerusalem formed a society that was totally void of any lack or poverty. When the apostles had the liberty to freely preach the grace of God and the power of the resurrection, a flood of loving-kindness, favor, and goodwill richly overflowed to every member of the church. Because of the great liberty in the church to freely preach the whole counsel of God, there wasn't one destitute or needy person in their midst.

Here, in the special wording of the Amplified Version of this text, we are allowed to see something extraordinary that was taking place. These believers were willing to release their proprietorship and personal ownership of their possessions in favor of establishing biblical stewardships with God. It is important to note that the money for this "common treasury" was *voluntarily funded* by the believers' generous giving, rather than being taken from them through religious arm-twisting, taxation, guilt trips, or other forms of unbiblical manipulation.

Notice carefully the words that the Holy Spirit chooses: *"…one by one, they brought (gave back) the amount received from the sales…"* (Acts 4:34). The important thing here is not the temporary communal lifestyle that some people overemphasize; rather, it is the fact that the believers "gave back" the amount they received from the sale of the possessions. Now, it is evident they did not "give back" the money to the apostles, for the apostles had no prior claim to the properties that were sold. However, God did, for He clearly states throughout His Word that the earth is His property, and the fullness of it is also His – that the cattle upon a thousand hills belong to Him as well as all the silver and gold.

> **For every beast of the forest is Mine, And the cattle on a thousand hills.**
>
> **Psalm 50:10**

> **"The silver is Mine, and the gold is Mine," says the LORD of hosts.**
>
> **Haggai 2:8**

This is true *stewardship*, when former proprietors give back to God that which had been under their control. How quickly poverty, lack, and insufficiency would leave the church of our day if its members would allow this early New Testament mindset of stewardship to once again predominate.

**All Of The Grace Of Giving
Must Come Out Of A Heart Of Love
And A Desire For God's Word
To Be Preached Around The World.**

# Man-Made Traditions Of Poverty

The devil has unrelentingly used the man-made traditions of poverty to maintain a false mindset among God's people that it is more spiritual to be poor than rich. These traditions make the Word of God of no effect.

> ...Thus you have made the commandment of God of no effect by your tradition. Hypocrites! Well did Isaiah prophesy about you, saying: "These people draw near to Me with their mouth, and honor Me with their lips, but their heart is far from Me. And in vain they worship Me, teaching as doctrines the commandments of men."
>
> **Matthew 15:6-9**

The enemy of the church knows the powerful influence that tradition can exert upon individuals. Traditions feed upon man's desire for homeostasis – the instinctive drive to find one's personal comfort level, and to be drawn irresistibly toward doing what one has always done to maintain the status quo and remain comfortable.

Man-made traditions also promote what I like to refer to as "psycho-sclerosis," or "hardening of the attitudes." It is the natural, fear-rooted tendency to fall in love with your own ideas, and then to vigorously defend them against anything new. It is romantic subjectivity that has nothing to do with the truth.

The good news is that, although the influence of tradition can be a daunting force within the lives of believers, the power of God's Word is much greater! By feeding the saints with the true bread of life (the unadulterated Word of God), there will come a rapid de-programming of the subconscious mindset of poverty that has attached itself to the Body of Christ.

# The True Riches Of The Church

The Bible confirms, throughout the Old and New Testaments, that the rich God of Heaven intended for His church to have all that they would need to fulfill His Great Commission. Jesus not only sent His church forward with the spiritual authority to fulfill His command (Matthew 28:18), but He also promised to provide His bride with all the natural resources she would need to fulfill His wishes.

But you shall be named the priests of the LORD, they shall call you the servants of our God. You shall eat the riches of the Gentiles, and in their glory you shall boast.

Isaiah 61:6

You will be called priests of the LORD, ministers of our God. You will be fed with the treasures of the nations and will boast in their riches. Instead of shame and dishonor, you will inherit a double portion of prosperity and everlasting joy.

Isaiah 61:6-7, *NLT*

God has abundantly provided every obedient believer with the following blessings (Deuteronomy 28:1-14):

- Blessed in the city and in the field (in every arena of life)
- Fruitful in your body
- Abounding in the production of your flocks and herds (money-making endeavors)
- Abounding in the bounty of your basket (your daily supply)
- Abounding in your storehouses (your savings accounts and investments)
- Victorious over all your enemies, causing those who come against you from one direction to flee from you in seven directions
- Successful in everything you set your hand to do
- Known throughout the land by the name of the Lord
- Abounding in the treasures of Heaven
- Lending your money but not having to borrow

- Ruling in life as the head and not the tail end of humanity
- Always coming out above; never ending up underneath

## The Good Bridegroom

It would most surely be abusive for a husband to neglect taking care of his wife. How much more offensive would it be if Jesus refused to take care of His bride? Jesus desires to provide a lavish banquet for His bride, a feast that includes all that His bride could ever need or desire. We can rejoice in the knowledge that King Jesus Christ, our wonderful Bridegroom, graciously supplies all that we need or desire, to become everything He has called us to be.

> **...His divine power has given to us all things that pertain to life and godliness, through the knowledge of Him who called us by glory and virtue.**
>
> **2 Peter 1:3**

> **...being confident of this very thing, that He who has begun a good work in you will complete it until the day of Jesus Christ.**
>
> **Philippians 1:6-7**

Just as a bridegroom pledges to his bride, "Everything I have also belongs to you," Jesus assures His church that His sacrifice at Calvary has secured her access to His divine inheritance. In the righteous and moral government of God, the church has a well-documented claim of joint ownership to all the riches of God's universe!

Husbands, likewise, dwell with them with understanding, giving honor to the wife, as to the weaker vessel, <u>and as being heirs together</u> of the grace of life...

1 Peter 3:7 [emphasis added]

The Spirit Himself bears witness with our spirit that we are children of God, <u>and if children, then heirs – heirs of God and joint heirs with Christ</u>...

Romans 8:16-17 [emphasis added]

Listen, my beloved brethren: Has God not chosen the poor of this world to be rich in faith and <u>heirs of the kingdom which He promised to those who love Him</u>?

James 2:5 [emphasis added]

## You Have A Divine Mission

As the blessed offspring of the rich God of Heaven, you will find that opportunities await you at every turn in the road. If you will allow the Spirit of God to operate in your heart, as it pertains to God's abundant supply for you and through you, then you will see an immediate change begin to take place in and around you.

### Prosperity Is Having Enough Of God's Provision To Fulfill The Assignment He Has Given You.

One of the reasons that God desires for you to prosper financially is so that you can be in a *position of influence* in this earth. Our rich God is fully aware that, in this world, money talks. It is time for the church of the Lord Jesus Christ to find her voice of influence and rise up with the financial clout of King's kids, so that the kingdoms of this world would become the kingdoms of our Lord and of His Christ!

> ...there were loud voices in heaven, saying, "The kingdoms of this world have become the kingdoms of our Lord and of His Christ, and He shall reign forever and ever!"
>
> **Revelation 11:15**

> ...through your descendants, all the nations of the earth will be blessed – all because you have obeyed me.
>
> **Genesis 22:18**, *NLT*

> Then all the nations of the world will see that you are a people claimed by the LORD, and they will stand in awe of you.
>
> **Deuteronomy 28:10**, *NLT*

## You Choose

It doesn't matter where you've come from or what has happened to you. If you want to prosper, then it is important to accept responsibility for the outcome of your life. Past issues may have fabricated wrong beliefs or forged negative habits, but the power of decision can transform your life.

## Prosperity Is Found In The Decision To Accept Personal Responsibility; The Enjoyment Of Your Future Is Hidden In Your Choices Of Today.

Friend, will you decide, today, to step into the rich inheritance of abundance that the Lord Jesus has purchased for you?

> **Now listen! Today I am giving you a choice between prosperity and disaster, between life and death...I call on heaven and earth to witness the choice you make. Oh, that you would choose life, that you and your descendants might live!**
>
> Deuteronomy 30:15, 19, *NLT*

Faithfulness Is Never Defined By The Standards Of Men, But Only By The Requirements Of Heaven.

Chapter 11

# FAITHFUL $TEWARDSHIP

Contrary to what some in the church believe, prosperity is not for prosperity's sake. God is calling us to be wise stewards of *His* wealth. Stewardship creates a new perception of prosperity and abundance. Stewards move into the unique position of having everything, while actually owning nothing.

God's stewards represent their Heavenly Father here on earth. He has given us the right to use the name of His Son, Jesus, by whose power and authority we carry out the royal business of the kingdom of God. When we take seriously our position as stewards, the abundant riches of Heaven start to flow toward us, to enable us to bring about the Father's plans.

> You didn't choose me! I chose you! I appointed you to go
> and produce lovely fruit always, so that no matter what you
> ask for from the Father, using my name, he will give it to you.
> **John 15:16, *TLB***

When you are operating in true stewardship, the divine favor of God will quickly cause things to start moving *for you* instead of *against you.* You will become the head and not the tail (Deuteronomy 28:13). You will begin to experience favor in every situation (Psalm 5:12). People who speak with you will feel as if they are speaking with the personal representative of the rich God of Heaven. Old enemies will grow powerless; their conflicts with you will diminish and even fade away.

> But you are a chosen generation, a royal priesthood, a holy nation, His own special people, that you may proclaim the praises of Him who called you out of darkness into His marvelous light.
>
> 1 Peter 2:9

> When a man's ways please the LORD, He makes even his enemies to be at peace with him.
>
> Proverbs 16:7

Those who are proper stewards of God walk in an ongoing communion and counsel with God.

> Blessed is the man who walks not in the counsel of the ungodly, Nor stands in the path of sinners, nor sits in the seat of the scornful; But his delight is in the law of the LORD, And in His law he meditates day and night. He shall be like a tree planted by the rivers of water, That brings forth its fruit in its season, whose leaf also shall not wither; And whatever he does shall prosper.
>
> Psalm 1:1-3

Thus says the LORD, your Redeemer, the Holy one of Israel: "I am the LORD your God, who teaches you to profit, Who leads you by the way you should go."

Isaiah 48:17

For as many as are led by the Spirit of God, these are sons of God. For you did not receive the spirit of bondage again to fear, but you received the Spirit of adoption by whom we cry out, "Abba, Father."

Romans 8:14-15

Proper stewards are quick to seek the Father's counsel and careful to apply His instructions. They understand that prosperity must be *received*, not achieved or pursued. Wise stewards don't go after things; they go after people, knowing that things will come.

# Stewards Redistribute God's Wealth

Stewards work for the purpose of *giving*. We do not work to prosper. We work to give, and we trust God to prosper. Our Heavenly Father is calling us to totally abandon the concept of being "givers to God." He wants us to become *redistributors* for God. When we set our hearts and minds on becoming a blessing, God removes the blinders, allowing us to see opportunities for advancing His kingdom.

> Let him who stole steal no longer, but rather let him labor, working with his hands what is good, that he may have something to give him who has need.
>
> Ephesians 4:28

The rich young ruler proved that he was working to prosper, not for the purpose of giving (Mark 10:17-22). He could not trust God in order to prosper, despite many Old Testament Scriptures that explained the blessings that would come to one who helped the poor.

> Blessed is he who considers the poor; The LORD will deliver him in time of trouble. The LORD will preserve him and keep him alive, And he will be blessed on the earth; You will not deliver him to the will of his enemies. The LORD will strengthen him on his bed of illness; You will sustain him on his sickbed.
>
> Psalm 41:1-3

> He who despises his neighbor sins; But he who has mercy on the poor, happy is he.
>
> Proverbs 14:21

> He who has pity on the poor lends to the LORD, And He will pay back what he has given.
>
> Proverbs 19:17

> He who gives to the poor will not lack, But he who hides his eyes will have many curses.
>
> Proverbs 28:27

Prosperity is in the heart, not in the pocketbook. In giving to help the poor, an individual is no longer looking at what is in it for him; he is considering others. It is in almsgiving – helping the poor – that a person's heart is changed into the heart of God.

## How God Feels About Your Gift

When you give to God, He knows your heartfelt attitude and the value you place on your offering. Because of this, *He* will feel the same way about your offering as *you* feel. God can never look upon something as being precious unless it is precious to you.

> **For we do not have a High Priest who cannot sympathize with our weaknesses, but was in all points tempted as we are, yet without sin.**
>
> **Hebrews 4:15**

> **And He looked up and saw the rich putting their gifts into the treasury, and He saw also a certain poor widow putting in two mites. So He said, "Truly I say to you that this poor widow has put in more than all; for all these out of their abundance have put in offerings for God, but she out of her poverty put in all the livelihood that she had."**
>
> **Luke 21:1-4**

We must always examine the motives for our giving, remembering that our gift is a seed, and seed always produces according to its kind (Genesis 1:11-12). In other words, the *motive* with which you sow will be multiplied back into your life. If you sow from selfish, prideful motives, then selfishness and pride will increase in your heart. If you sow from love, gratitude, and obedience, then those godly characteristics will be multiplied with every seed you sow.

There are three possible motivations for giving:

• **Wanting to be seen**

Therefore, when you do a charitable deed, do not sound a trumpet before you as the hypocrites do in the synagogues and in the streets, that they may have glory from men. Assuredly, I say to you, they have their reward.

Matthew 6:2

• **Wanting to be known**

Thus, whenever you give to the poor, do not blow a trumpet before you, as the hypocrites in the synagogues and in the streets like to do, that they may be recognized and honored and praised by men. Truly I tell you, they have their reward in full already.

Matthew 6:2, AMP

• **Loving obedience**

So Samuel said: "Has the LORD as great delight in burnt offerings and sacrifices, as in obeying the voice of the LORD? Behold, to obey is better than sacrifice, and to heed than the fat of rams."

1 Samuel 15:22

All of the grace of giving must come out of *a heart of love and a desire for God's Word to be preached around the world.* A true believer already has the heart of a giver. He is eager to become a

redistribution center for God. If he becomes stingy and fearful with money, it is because he is being taught to be that way (often by other believers who do not understand the concept of stewardship). Remember, God always views your gift in the same way you do.

## The Foolish vs. The Faithful Steward

The primary difference between a foolish steward and a faithful steward is that of focus. A foolish steward is focused on himself and his own desires, whereas the faithful steward is focused on fulfilling the desires of his master. Let's examine a few ways that this manifests in a person's actions:

- Stewards sow; the foolish hoard.
- Stewards focus on blessing others; the foolish accumulate blessings for themselves.
- Stewards shun debt; the foolish embrace debt.
- Stewards give; the foolish grasp.
- Stewards are content to be managers of God's assets; the foolish strive to manage their own assets.
- Stewards seek to please God and fulfill His purposes; the foolish seek to please themselves and gratify their own desires.

You cannot successfully dedicate yourself to another's well-being while competing with him for your own well-being. A proper steward must have a singleness of purpose in carrying out his master's business.

> But indeed for this purpose I have raised you up, that I
> may show My power in you, and that My name may be de-
> clared in all the earth.
>
> Exodus 9:16

## Singleness Of Purpose – Not Control

It's sad, but true, that the state or municipality in which you
live today understands more about stewardship than the average
Christian does.

> So the master commended the unjust steward because
> he had dealt shrewdly. For the sons of this world are more
> shrewd in their generation than the sons of light.
>
> Luke 16:8

> ...it is true that the citizens of this world are more
> shrewd than the godly are.
>
> Luke 16:8, *NLT*

Every successful person must lay up some amount, from day
to day, in order to meet the accumulating monthly costs of living.
The stewardship of God's kingdom is no different. There is only
one way to live successfully and not lay up any treasures on earth.
That is by totally giving over to God any and all assets you now
control and choosing to become His steward.

Stewardship and prosperity are lived on three levels:

• Obedience – The tithe (Ten percent of all that you receive)

- Being led by the Holy Spirit – The offerings
- Purpose – To be like God (To be a giver and redistribute God's wealth)

> **For God so loved the world that He gave His only begotten Son, that whoever believes in Him should not perish but have everlasting life.**
>
> **John 3:16**

> **And as He spoke, a certain Pharisee asked Him to dine with him. So He went in and sat down to eat. When the Pharisee saw it, he marveled that He had not first washed before dinner. Then the Lord said to him, "Now you Pharisees make the outside of the cup and dish clean, but your inward part is full of greed and wickedness. Foolish ones! Did not He who made the outside make the inside also? But rather give alms of such things as you have; then indeed all things are clean to you."**
>
> **Luke 11:37-41**

Like the Pharisees in the above Scripture passage, thousands outwardly present themselves as generous and obedient to God, yet inwardly, they are full of selfishness and greed. They claim to be believers, yet they have not fulfilled even the first step of obedient stewardship: the tithe. Tithing is the most primary, elemental level of godly stewardship. One cannot expect to even *enter* the realm of God's prosperity unless he is a tither. Why? Because the tithe opens the windows of Heaven.

> **"Will a man rob God? Yet you have robbed Me! But you say, 'In what way have we robbed You?' <u>In tithes and offerings</u>.**

You are cursed with a curse, for you have robbed Me, Even this whole nation. "Bring all the tithes into the storehouse, That there may be food in My house, And try Me now in this," says the LORD of hosts, "If I will not open for you the windows of heaven And pour out for you such blessing That there will not be room enough to receive it. And I will rebuke the devourer for your sakes, So that he will not destroy the fruit of your ground, Nor shall the vine fail to bear fruit for you in the field... And all nations will call you blessed, for you will be a delightful land," Says the LORD of hosts.

**Malachi 3:8-12 [emphasis added]**

And all the tithe of the land, whether of the seed of the land or of the fruit of the tree, is the LORD's. It is holy to the LORD.

**Leviticus 27:30**

## Those who tithe demonstrate four things:

- They are obedient in financial matters.
- The wealth they receive is not their own, for it comes from the Master of their stewardship.
- Heaven will remain open, so that their Master will be able to prosper all they do.
- Faithfulness in tithing also stops the devourer from diminishing the harvest of their stewardship. (The devourer is not Satan – it is the broken washing machine, the increased gas prices, etc. – the unexpected things that steal your finances.)

As stewards, we must keep in mind that when we bring the tithe to God, we are **not giving** Him a gift. Since the tithe already belongs to the Lord, we cannot "give" it to Him. (If it is already His, then it is not a gift.)

But, friend, when we examine Malachi 3:8 above, we discover that more than the tithe belongs to God. Being that it is impossible to rob someone of that which doesn't already belong to him, we have to conclude that if we were robbing God of the offering, then the offering must also belong to Him. Everything that comes under our control already does, and always will, belong to God!

> **The earth is the LORD's, and all its fullness, The world and those who dwell therein.**
>
> Psalms 24:1

We must learn to stop looking upon offering time as a giving experience. We must start seeing it as it really is, an *opportunity to invest and redistribute God's wealth*. It is an unchanging truth that if we try to hold on to the assets under our control, treating them as if they were our own, we will interrupt the flow of God's blessing into our lives.

## The Tithe Opens The Windows Of Heaven; The Offering Determines What Comes Out Of Those Windows.

The final level of stewardship is *purpose*. We must continually ask ourselves, "What is the purpose of my heart when I tithe? What is the purpose of my heart when I give?" The Pharisees were tithing, but God called them hypocrites because their attitude was not one of justice, mercy, and faith (Matthew 23:23). *God wants our hearts*.

> If you are willing and obedient, you shall eat the good of
> the land; But if you refuse and rebel, you shall be devoured
> by the sword...
>
> Isaiah 1:19-20

> "And now, O priests, this commandment is for you. If you
> will not hear, and if you will <u>not take it to heart</u>, To give glory
> to My name," says the LORD of hosts, "I will send a curse
> upon you, and I will curse your blessings. Yes, I have cursed
> them already, <u>because you do not take it to heart</u>."
>
> Malachi 2:1-2 [emphasis added]

For all of these men of God, the curse came because of their
words and their heart attitudes, not because of their money.

## The Mammon System

Even though the wealth that God places in your hands does
not belong to you, you will still be required to make wise decisions
as to how you use it. The world we live in presents countless
"opportunities" for wealth consumption. Actually, the present
system of commerce, based on the practice of lending with
interest, is, in fact, an expanded form of the ancient Mesopotamian
"mammon system."

Satan cleverly employs the mammon system of this world to
keep you in the bondage of debt, so that God cannot freely make
withdrawals from the finances He entrusts to your keeping. Every
steward who wishes to properly accomplish God's will, with his
finances, must make a quality decision to get out of debt.

# Beware Of Covetousness

The steward who proves to be uncompromisingly obedient when he has very little will soon be trusted with much. Allowing God to freely make any and all withdrawals He desires from your account brings with it the assurance from God's Word that He will steadily make bountiful deposits back into your stewardship account. As your need for surplus increases, God promises to increase your harvest each time you sow!

> He who is faithful in what is least is faithful also in much; and he who is unjust in what is least is unjust also in much.
>
> **Luke 16:10**

> For God is the one who gives seed to the farmer and then bread to eat. In the same way, he will give you many opportunities to do good, and he will produce a great harvest of generosity in you. Yes, you will be enriched so that you can give even more generously. And when we take your gifts to those who need them, they will break out in thanksgiving to God.
>
> **2 Corinthians 9:10-11,** *NLT*

As God enriches us with increasing abundance and prosperity, we must remember that we are stewards, not owners. The spiritually mature children of the rich God never have a desire to possess the riches He allows them to control. A true steward of God is well aware of the warning Jesus gave every believer:

> "Take heed and beware of covetousness, for one's life does not consist in the abundance of the things he possesses."
>
> **Luke 12:15**

Abraham understood that the wealth God had placed under his control wasn't his to store up strictly for his own personal use. It all belonged to God.

> Now the LORD had said to Abram: "Get out of your country, from your family, and from your father's house, to a land that I will show you. I will make you a great nation; I will bless you and make your name great; and you shall be a blessing. I will bless those who bless you, and I will curse him who curses you; and in you all the families of the earth shall be blessed."
>
> **Genesis 12:1-3**

A close examination of God's Word will reveal that God has not called His children to be the owners of their own private hoard of assets. He has called them to be faithful stewards over the assets He places on assignment with them. He desires to give His children all things, when He knows that their foremost desire is to please Heaven.

> ...seek first the kingdom of God and His righteousness, and all these things shall be added to you.
>
> **Matthew 6:33**

## The Riches Of God's Glory

Rich children enjoy their Father's riches. God desires to put into your hands *the glory*, or the actual wealth of His infinite riches, enabling you to properly function as His well-funded steward. It is nothing more than religious tradition that demands that you wait until you get to Heaven to enjoy the riches of God's kingdom.

The riches of God's glory are for you, right now. Because of Jesus' sacrifice, God has equipped you with His own nature, His mind, and His power, which He wants you to use to their full potential, to bring you into all the wealth and prosperity you will ever need. God wants you, as His blood-bought child, to:

- Live in the divine health that Jesus Christ secured for you.

- See others healed through the power God releases through you.

- Walk with peace in your heart and mind.

- Have the victory over every attack the devil dares to send your way.

- Have a totally new anointing that will move you into the victory, each and every time you step out on behalf of God and His kingdom.

- Have more than enough of everything to be blessed and to be a blessing to all the families of the earth.

- One day enter into Heaven, to hear the greatest words any human being could ever hear: "Well done, good and faithful steward."

# Obedience Is The Master Key That Unlocks Heaven's Abundance.

Chapter 12

# A FRESH
# $TART

Your rich Father is eager to see you step into the life that He has already provided for you through the supreme sacrifice of His Son, Jesus Christ. This life is a gift from our generous Father. It is both abundant life now and eternal life throughout the endless ages.

I would like to review some of the information we have discussed and equip you with *24 Keys* designed to free you from the grips of poverty and lack, to catapult you into the riches of your inheritance, and to transform you into a faithful, influential steward of the Master's resources.

## 24 Keys Leading To The God Kind Of Life

**Key #1:**
**You must always tithe.** *(Leviticus 27:30, Malachi 3:10)*
**Poverty Is Not The Lack Of Money; Poverty Is The Proof Of Misguided Money.**

> There is one who scatters, yet increases more; And there is one who withholds more than is right, But it leads to poverty. The generous soul will be made rich, And he who waters will also be watered himself.
>
> Proverbs 11:24-25

## Key #2:
## You must keep right priorities. *(James 4:3, Matt. 6:33)*

Wrong priorities sabotage the man who is in search of prosperity. Be sure to give God the firstfruits, and don't forget His commands (Deuteronomy 8:11-18).

**What You Do First Determines How Life Will Respond.**

> Honor the LORD with your possessions, And with the firstfruits of all your increase; So your barns will be filled with plenty, And your vats will overflow with new wine.
>
> Proverbs 3:9-10

## Key #3:
## You must refuse double-mindedness.

> But let him ask in faith, with no doubting, for he who doubts is like a wave of the sea driven and tossed by the wind. For let not that man suppose that he will receive anything from the Lord; he is a double-minded man, unstable in all his ways.
>
> James 1:6-8

## Key #4:
## Your offerings must be acceptable in God's sight.

> For if there is first a willing mind, it is accepted according to what one has, and not according to what he does not have.
>
> 2 Corinthians 8:12

## Key #5:
## You must pursue proper understanding. *(Matthew 7:7-8)*

> Beloved, I pray that you may prosper in all things and be in health, just as your soul prospers.
>
> 3 John 2

## Key #6:
## You must turn aside all fear.

> For God has not given us a spirit of fear, but of power and of love and of a sound mind.
>
> 2 Timothy 1:7

> Casting down arguments and every high thing that exalts itself against the knowledge of God, bringing every thought into captivity to the obedience of Christ.
>
> 2 Corinthians 10:5

## Key #7:
## You must remain in faith.

> Now faith is the substance of things hoped for, the evidence of things not seen...But without faith it is impossible to please Him, for he who comes to God must believe that He is, and that He is a rewarder of those who diligently seek Him.
>
> **Hebrews 11:1, 6**

> ...According to your faith let it be to you.
>
> **Matthew 9:29**

## Key #8:
## You must destroy all unbelief.

> And they overcame him by the blood of the Lamb and by the word of their testimony, and they did not love their lives to the death.
>
> **Revelation 12:11**

## Key #9:
## You must never look back to your old life.

In order to walk in abundance, we have to disconnect from past relationships and embrace the relationships of tomorrow. A life without harvest is proof that you have invested in the wrong people.

> But Jesus said to him, "No one, having put his hand to the plow, and looking back, is fit for the kingdom of God."
>
> **Luke 9:62**

## Key #10:
## If married, you must maintain your marriage according to Heaven's Guidelines.

> Wives, likewise, be submissive to your own husbands...
>
> 1 Peter 3:1

> Husbands, likewise, dwell with them with understanding, giving honor to the wife, as to the weaker vessel, and as being heirs together of the grace of life, that your prayers may not be hindered.
>
> 1 Peter 3:7

## Key #11:
## You must maintain a proper relationship with your spiritual leaders.

> Obey those who rule over you, and be submissive, for they watch out for your souls, as those who must give account. Let them do so with joy and not with grief, for that would be unprofitable for you.
>
> Hebrews 13:17

## Key #12:
## You must maintain a loving life.

> Therefore if you bring your gift to the altar, and there remember that your brother has something against you, leave your gift there before the altar, and go your way. First be reconciled to your brother, and then come and offer your gift.
>
> Matthew 5:23-24

## Key #13:
## You must try, prove and believe the proven ministries of God.

> ...Believe in the LORD your God, and you shall be established; believe His prophets, and you shall prosper.
>
> 2 Chronicles 20:20

## Key #14:
## You must be willing to work. *(Prov. 10:4-5, 12:24, 13:4; Eph. 4:28)*
**All Men Want To Be Rich, But Few Men Want To Go To Work.**

> ...If anyone will not work, neither shall he eat.
>
> 2 Thessalonians 3:10

**The Problems You Solve Determine The Rewards You Receive.**

## Key #15:
## You must keep sin out of your life.

> Now it shall come to pass, if you diligently obey the voice of the LORD your God, to observe carefully all His commandments which I command you today, that the LORD your God will set you high above all nations of the earth. And all these blessings shall come upon you and overtake you, because you obey the voice of the LORD your God.
>
> Deuteronomy 28:1-2

The pathway to prosperity must include the decision to pursue personal excellence. Your pursuit of personal excellence awakens the process of transformation, and it is only proven by the attitude with which you face the giant named "Maintenance." Why is this true? Because excellence is a journey, not a destination.

**Today's Excellence Is Tomorrow's Mediocrity.**

> Do you see a man who excels in his work? He will stand before kings; He will not stand before unknown men.
>
> Proverbs 22:29

## Key #16:
## You must choose and use your words wisely.

> For assuredly, I say to you, whoever says to this mountain, "Be removed and be cast into the sea," and does not doubt in his heart, but believes that those things he says will be done, he will have whatever he says.
>
> Mark 11:23

## Key #17:
## You must faithfully pay your vows to God.

> When you make a vow to God, do not delay to pay it; For He has no pleasure in fools. Pay what you have vowed.
>
> Ecclesiastes 5:4

## Key #18:
## You must keep the Lord in His rightful place...and maintain a right perception of God.

> The LORD is my shepherd; I shall not want.
>
> Psalm 23:1

The pathway to prosperity must include the decision to be grateful. Be grateful for what you have, and don't be sad over what you don't (Hebrews 13:15, Colossians 3:15, Philippians 4:11-12).

## Key #19:
## You must never love money.

> For the love of money is a root of all kinds of evil, for which some have strayed from the faith in their greediness, and pierced themselves through with many sorrows.

> 1 Timothy 6:10

## Key #20:
## You must respond to the cries of the poor.

> Whoever shuts his ears to the cry of the poor will also cry himself and not be heard.

> Proverbs 21:13

## Key #21:
## You must be a faithful doer of God's Word.

> ...be doers of the word, and not hearers only, deceiving yourselves...he who looks into the perfect law of liberty and continues in it, and is not a forgetful hearer but a doer of the work, this one will be blessed in what he does.

> James 1:22, 25

## Key #22:
## You must rid yourself of traditional thinking.

> ...you have made the commandment of God of no effect by your tradition.

> Matthew 15:6

## Key #23:
## You must learn and exercise patience.

> And He said, "The kingdom of God is as if a man should scatter seed on the ground, and should sleep by night and rise by day, and the seed should sprout and grow, he himself does not know how. For the earth yields crops by itself: first the blade, then the head, after that the full grain in the head."
>
> Mark 4:26-28

## Key #24:
## Remember, the best harvest is always saved for last.
*(Matthew 25:31-40)*

> ...you yourselves are our letter of recommendation (our credentials), written in your hearts, to be known (perceived, recognized) and read by everybody.
>
> 2 Corinthians 3:2, *AMP*

## Four Key Decisions In Life

Future prosperity is intricately tied to present decisions. Allow me to share four key decisions that will radically affect your ability to receive God's abundance in life:

**1. Your decision to embrace the Word of God as the infallible final authority in life** (Psalm 19:7-11)

> Sanctify them by Your truth. Your Word is truth.
>
> John 17:17

In 2 Chronicles 1:11-12, Solomon asked for God's wisdom, and as a result, he gained wealth. *God's Word is His wisdom.* God judges your love for Him by your love of His truth. You will invest time into what you love. Your relationship with God can be no deeper than your relationship with His Word.

## The Proof Of Respect Is The Investment Of Time.

### 2. Your decision to honor authority

**And we urge you, brethren, to recognize those who labor among you, and are over you in the Lord and admonish you, and to esteem them very highly in love for their work's sake. Be at peace among yourselves.**

**1 Thessalonians 5:12-13**

Whether it's a boss, a parent, or the shepherd of the house, Honor is the seed to access. Dishonor will disconnect you from all that is good in life.

## Honor Is Proven By Obedience.

### 3. Your decision to discover and complete your assignment, regardless of the cost (1 Chronicles 28:20, 2 Timothy 4:7-8, Luke 9:51, 62)

But none of these things move me; nor do I count my life dear to myself, so that I may finish my race with joy, and the ministry which I received from the Lord Jesus, to testify to the gospel of the grace of God.

Acts 20:24

Do you have any idea where God would take you if you simply knew how to act when you got there? The Law of Character says that character is the foundation upon which your life's work is built.

## Your Life Is Not Determined By Your Position But By Your Disposition.

**4. Your decision to choose right associations**

He who walks with wise men will be wise, but the companion of fools will be destroyed.

Proverbs 13:20

## To Achieve Success, You Must Follow On The Path Of Someone Who Has Already Walked There.

*Remember, there are three types of people in your life:*

- **Compromisers:** Those who are relentless at trying to get you to compromise your newly built standards: "It's okay, you don't have to be so stiff and rigid all the time." (Past friends, acquaintances, etc.)

- **Companions:** Those who are neither good nor bad for your future. It is nearly impossible to tell their effect. (Friends, family, the fun people – but they may be taking you nowhere.)

- **Committed:** Those who are adamantly committed to a lifetime of success for you and yours.

As you embrace and follow these powerful keys and principles, you will see the chains of lack and poverty fall away. The wealth of your rich God will finally begin to flow through your life, supplying you with more than enough to complete the assignment He has given you!

Honor
Is The
Doorway
Through
Which All
Prosperity
Walks.

Conclusion

# OUR ONE AMBITION

Friend, we have been placed on this earth for one purpose: to please and bring glory to our God! (Revelation 4:11, *KJV*; Isaiah 43:7) You may find yourself asking, "How could I, a meager man, bring pleasure to a rich God who already has everything and owns the cattle on a thousand hills? What can I do that could possibly bring Him pleasure?"

## God's Greatest Pleasure Is To Be Believed.

Do you believe the good news of abundance and prosperity that I have shared from God's Word? Understand, friend, you bring your Father great pleasure when you believe and act upon the following truths:

- Your God is a rich God.

- God's son, Jesus, left the riches of Heaven and sacrificed His life to purchase abundant, eternal life for you.

- You are a joint heir, with Christ, of all the lavish, extravagant wealth of your rich Father; it is your blood-bought inheritance.

- As you continually meditate on the promises of God's Word, your way of thinking will change; prosperity will develop inside of you.

- By operating in the biblical precepts of financial wisdom, your rich Father will make you a steward of more than enough wealth to complete the assignment that He has given you.

- You can bring pleasure and glory to God and His kingdom by embracing your God-given stewardship and by using your wealth to finance the gospel around the world.

## Blessed To Be A Blessing

Your first response to every good gift that comes to you should always be to give thanks to your Heavenly Father for the trust He has demonstrated in you by placing it into your care. Faithful stewards always give their rich Heavenly Father praise for every good and perfect gift He bestows on them.

The next thing you should do is to automatically ask God this question: *"Lord, have you released this new asset to me for sowing, or is it for me and my loved ones to use for a season?"* When you set your heart and mind on becoming a blessing, God removes the blinders, allowing you to see opportunities for advancing His kingdom.

## A Bountiful, Cheerful Sower
## Will Abound With Many Blessings.

(2 Corinthians 9:6)

As you faithfully follow the principle of thanksgiving and then ask your Heavenly Father to reveal His plan for each asset, you will always keep your motivation in line with God's purposes for your life.

## What You Cast Upon The Waters Of Heaven
## Shall Return To The Shores Of Your Life.

(Ecclesiastes 11:1)

# Releasing God's Assets

The instant you achieve prosperity is the instant that money is no longer the driving force behind your decisions. Passion (fueled by your gratitude and desire to help others achieve) is now your driving force. It is important to understand that really successful stewards are always willing to release anything they have at God's command. Proverbs 11:25 reminds us: *"The generous soul will be made rich, and he who waters will also be watered himself."*

## Generosity Is The Proof
## That You Have Conquered Greed.

Take a moment and inventory your goods. Do you have some seed in your barn that is just sitting there, inactive and unproductive? (Keep in mind that God most certainly wants His children to have savings accounts as well as retirement accounts. See Deuteronomy 28:5, 1 Timothy 5:8, and Proverbs 13:22.) Be sensitive to the voice of your Master, accurately discerning how He wants His assets redistributed. As you listen for His directions, you will be filled with the joy and excitement of knowing that you are a kingdom-multiplying tool in the hand of your God!

Here are five important steps to bringing pleasure to our rich God:

1. **Make a quality decision, today, to become faithful to your God in all things!**

   And the things that you have heard from me among many witnesses, commit these to faithful men who will be able to teach others also.

   **2 Timothy 2:2**

2. **Become faithful in small amounts.**

   ...Well done, good and faithful servant; you have been faithful over a few things, I will make you ruler over many things. Enter into the joy of your lord.

   **Matthew 25:23**

3. **Prove yourself extra careful in money matters.**

   Moreover it is required in stewards that one be found faithful.

   **1 Corinthians 4:2**

**4. Prove yourself faithful in that which belongs to others.**

> And if you have not been faithful in what is another man's, who will give you what is your own?
>
> Luke 16:12

**5. Be a cheerful, prompt-to-do-it giver.**

> ...He who sows sparingly will also reap sparingly, and he who sows bountifully will also reap bountifully. So let each one give as he purposes in his heart, not grudgingly or of necessity; for God loves a cheerful giver. And God is able to make all grace abound toward you, that you, always having all sufficiency in all things, may have an abundance for every good work.
>
> 2 Corinthians 9:6-8

# Your Prosperity Brings God Pleasure

As you prove to be an obedient and faithful steward of the Master's funds, you will see those funds abundantly multiply. The surplus that will come forth from a properly operated stewardship will make it easy for you to demonstrate to the world how good your rich Father really is.

> Let your light so shine before men, that they may see your good works and glorify your Father in heaven.
>
> Matthew 5:16

As we have repeatedly seen, Scripture openly declares that our rich God delights in bestowing riches upon His offspring. Scripture also tells us that it pleases God when we tell others about the joy He receives by prospering us.

> **...And let them [the children of God] say continually, "Let the LORD be magnified, Who has pleasure in the prosperity of His servant."**
>
> **Psalm 35:27**

If God's children strictly enacted this verse, we would continually be telling people how much God really wants all of us to prosper. Sadly, in today's atmosphere of traditional religious teachings, those who say too much about God's desire to prosper His children are often branded as heretics.

Remember that God has given you the ability to prosper. You can reach a dying world with the good news if you use that prosperity correctly. We need to circle the globe with the good news that Jesus died on the cross to save us!

If we keep living according to our old concepts – our old ideas about money and prosperity – there is no way we will ever reach the lost. It will take a breakthrough in our lives, and in the lives of thousands of other believers, to fully experience God's abundance and begin to reach the world.

Put these principles to work in your life today and begin to experience your breakthrough. God wants you to live the good life and have more than enough to finance the gospel around the world!

It is now time for all believers to take a bold step forward and start thoroughly trusting and believing God's Word, as it declares His desire to abundantly supply us with all blessings. To get started, all we need to do is drop all of those old traditions of poverty, and then boldly decide to believe all the promises of God, without compromise. Just give it a try and see how quickly the biblical promise of prosperity begins to manifest itself in your life!

> **Trust in the LORD, and do good; Dwell in the land, and feed on His faithfulness. Delight yourself also in the LORD, And He shall give you the desires of your heart. Commit your way to the LORD, Trust also in Him, And He shall bring it to pass. He shall bring forth your righteousness as the light, And your justice as the noonday. Rest in the LORD, and wait patiently for Him; Do not fret because of him who prospers in his way, Because of the man who brings wicked schemes to pass.**
>
> **Psalm 37:3-7**

> **I have been young, and now am old; Yet I have not seen the righteous forsaken, Nor his descendants begging bread. He is ever merciful, and lends; And his descendants are blessed.**
>
> **Psalm 37:25-26**

I invite you to come into full agreement with the things you have learned in this book, and earnestly pray the following prayer.

*"Lord Jesus, I give you praise for the riches you have laid up for me. I thank you for supplying all my needs in accordance with your riches in glory. I claim every one of your promises, knowing that you will properly bless me as one of your children, prospering me beyond anything I could ever think or ask. By faith, I believe that you will place your desires into my heart, and as I commit my ways to you, you will bring every one of those God-given desires to pass, so that I may properly glorify you as a faithful steward of your kingdom. Amen."*

# ABOUT
# THE AUTHOR

Author of more than eighteen compelling books, numerous magazine articles, and countless audio and video resources, Dr. Robb Thompson is an exceptionally skilled relational and leadership strategist. In addition, he is the Vice Chairman of The Gabriel Call, a ministry dedicated to raising and training entrepreneurs to fund the gospel through the local church; President and Founder of the Dan EL Institute of Higher Learning, an online Christian college dedicated to equipping tomorrow's leaders; and a motivational speaker to businesses and corporations around the world.

## Discover other titles by Robb Thompson:

The Elephant In The Room

The Ten Critical Laws Of Relationship

Everyday Ways To Enjoy Success At Work

## Connect with Me Online:

Twitter: http://twitter.com/robbthompson

Facebook: http://www.facebook.com/robbdthompson

# The Harrison House Vision

Proclaiming the truth and the power

Of the Gospel of Jesus Christ

With excellence;

Challenging Christians to

Live victoriously,

Grow spiritually,

Know God intimately.